2001: A POETRY ODYSSEY WEST LANCASHIRE

Edited by Dave Thomas

First published in Great Britain in 2001 by
YOUNG WRITERS
Remus House,
Coltsfoot Drive,
Peterborough, PE2 9JX
Telephone (01733) 890066

HB ISBN 0 75432 970 4
SB ISBN 0 75432 971 2

FOREWORD

Young Writers was established in 1991 with the aim to promote creative writing in children, to make reading and writing poetry fun.

This year the 2001: A Poetry Odyssey competition again proved to be a tremendous success with over 50,000 entries received nationwide.

The amount of hard work and effort put into each entry impressed us all, and is reflective of the teaching skills in schools today.

The task of selecting poems for publication was a difficult one but nevertheless, an enjoyable experience. We hope you are as pleased with the final selection in *2001: A Poetry Odyssey West Lancashire* as we are.

CONTENTS

Stephanie Coole	86
Leanne Ralph	86
Shaun Thompson	87
Gary Nicholls	88
Tracey Olsen	88
Suzi Jones	89
Megan Speakman	90
Matthew Postlethwaite	91
Vicky Caine	92
Mark Livesey	92
Lindsay Milner	93
Rebecca Hems	94
Jonathan Lomax	95
Leann Martin	96
Lee Collinson	96
Natalie Whitehead	97
Jade Robinson	97
Jennifer Milburn	98
Chris Pendlebury	99
Zoe Hill	100
Mai-Yee Chan	100
Matthew Barnes	101
Sarah Jones	101
Rachael Thompson	102
Megan Edwards	102
Jenny Conchie	103
John Watkins	104
Kaylie Brocklehurst	104
Jade Hamer	105
Andrew Flanagan	106
Sarah Anderson	106
Emma Purvis	107
Allia Howard	107
Scott A Silburn	108
Lauren Oldland	109
Thomas Higgins	109
Sean Hamer	110
Mark Wright	110

The Poems

THE MERMAID

A mermaid sat upon a sandy rock,
Her eyes gleamed soft and green.
Come, come, come with me,
To the land beneath the sea.

Her tail gleamed in the heat of the sun,
As we dived in the rolling waves.
We swam through the deep blue sea,
And entered into the mermaid's cave.

The walls glistened with shining jewels,
She beckoned for me to follow.
We glided swiftly through the dazzling tunnels,
But stopped when we reached a small burrow.

I gazed downwards to see what was there,
A huddle of mermaids all toiling.
A cauldron in the centre on a three-legged chair.
A red potion inside boiling.

A mermaid escorted me inside so fair,
And plunged me into the poisonous substance.
The mermaids all chanted like one single voice,
Then a flash that could blind you in an instance.

My legs felt a strange tingling sensation,
I saw that I had grown a tail!
My short black hair became long and flowing,
And I could swim as smoothly as a whale.

For I too had become a mermaid,
Living with them in the deep blue sea.
Swimming amongst the shoals of fish,
Eating seaweed cake for my tea!

Emily Glover (12)
Burscough Priory High School

MY SPECIAL AUTUMN FRIEND!

Walking in the park one day,
Listening to the birds.
On the trees the autumn leaves,
Dance in the sky.
The gold the red,
They float down above me.

There is no path; it's full of leaves,
They blow about like feathers.
What pretty shapes they are,
Sharp ones,
Crunchy ones,
They are all beautiful.

I say to myself, 'What can I do?'
Then a tree bent down and said,
'Why don't we play catch across that field'
'Yes let's go and play.'

We played and played,
But then I got tired.
So I went home to bed,
And dreamt about my friend the tree,
My special friend called *Fred!*

Kelly Baldwin (12)
Burscough Priory High School

OUR DOG'S BREATH

People think our dogs are cute,
But when they bend down
They put on a frown and
Feel as if they're about to puke!

Like dragons' breath, theirs could probably kill you,
Although they don't breathe fire,
But especially when they're tired,
Their breath is lethal to you.

Catherine Rocca (12)
Burscough Priory High School

JIMMY

Jimmy, my invisible friend,
He moves like the wind.
My sister, she hates him,
She'd rather have him binned.

My sister thinks I'm crazy,
She thinks I'm made of wood.
She could believe in him you know,
If she could see him she could.

Jimmy is my mate,
Whether things are good or bad,
Jimmy will brighten up your day,
Even when he's sad.

Jimmy is a loyal dog,
Will always stand by my side.
Well maybe not always,
Will he ever die?

I'm 12 now and Jimmy has gone,
He's gone and left my home.
Just like a loving mother,
Loving wherever he may roam.

Simon Tonge (12)
Burscough Priory High School

THE HERON

How majestic the heron stands,
Tall in splendour, towering high,
He takes to the sky flying far and wide,
As he glides above the shimmering lake,
In pursuit of food that he must take,
He spots his prey and what a dish,
He swoops to snatch a tasty fish.

He flies back to his nest and settles down to rest,
As the darkness falls all around, the heron makes not a sound,
He tucks his head beneath his wing,
And as dawn does break and the birds do sing,
Once again the heron rises,
Not knowing of the surprises.

He spreads his wings and starts his flight,
And goes in search of a delicious pike,
He goes the wrong way, it's not the same,
He stands before this standing lane,
It swirls and bends with beeping horns,
He runs across towards the corn.

He's lost, oh no, without a friend,
He darts back to the other end,
He finds his home and what a morning,
I'll never do that, he says, whilst yawning,
But wait until the adjoining day.

Alyson Browne (12)
Burscough Priory High School

MY BIKE

I got a bike for Christmas
529 pounds
I ride it every day
I think it's really sound.

It's got full suspension
Disc brakes front and back
27 gears
I ride it on my mate's bike track.

When I'm racing around the block
I pedal really fast
But if it's against my older friends
I usually come last.

It has a mud guard at the front
It keeps me free of dirt
It doesn't get onto my shorts
Or onto my shirt.

Whilst I'm riding along a track
I stop to pull a wheeley
Then I come down on to the ground
And then ride off quite freely.

It's the Barracuda Kamikaze
The green one, you know
You want to know where I got it from?
Barracuda and Co.

Michael Weingart (12)
Burscough Priory High School

THE HOUSE IN THE MIDDLE OF THE JUNGLE!

The house in the middle of the jungle,
Is the house of a very old woman.
The house in the middle of the jungle,
Was baked in a rusty old oven!

The house in the middle of the jungle.
Is like it is lost on its own.
The house in the middle of the jungle,
Looks like it is made out of creased old stone!

The animals are creeping slowly towards,
The house that is lost on its own.
They creep inside with enormous paws,
To eat from the wardens home!

This woman, who I forgot to say.
Is like a warden who cares for her friends,
She feeds them all through day and through the night,
Until the happiness ends.

And when it ends, there is more.
As the warden has to leave.
She has no more food left in her store,
The animals have to eat what they please.

Poor, desperate creatures,
Hungry and thirsty for food.
They want their warden back for good,
But all they want is her food.

The house in the middle of the jungle,
Was a very happy time.
Before the warden left she said,
The animals will always be mine.

Lauren Gaskell (12)
Burscough Priory High School

THE MIDNIGHT FEAST

My stomach as empty as the ocean deep,
Awoke me from my beauty sleep,
I slipped away from dreamy land,
To put some food into my hand.

Slowly out through the door,
Across the cold dark creeping floor,
I tiptoed like a hunting beast,
Out to get my midnight feast.

Past my parents' room, quiet as a mouse,
Careful not to wake the whole house,
Across the landing, facing the stairs,
Now I must quickly and quietly submerge.

Across the hall now, don't wake the dogs,
Soon I'll get my chocolate logs,
I'm in the kitchen now, no time to waste,
There's lots of food that I must taste.

The fridge is open the food is mine,
But I'll have to eat it in double the time,
There is a cake up on high,
Can I reach it? It won't hurt to try.

The cake is gone; I ate it with ease,
But oh what's this? A nice piece of cheese,
The cheese is gone,
Now back to bed, no time for a scone.

But Mum is here, angry as a beast,
Here to punish me for my midnight feast,
Then I awoke with a scream,
Just to find out it was only a dream.

Lee Henry (12)
Burscough Priory High School

INSPIRATION

You sit there in lessons,
Entranced in it all.
But when they hand you the poem,
You take your eye off the ball.

> The poem seeps in and blocks everything out.
> Even when the teacher begins to shout.
> I sit like an ice cube,
> Stuck to my chair. The locked gate was the table,
> The key was not there.

I have entered the poem to steal some ideas,
But what will I find? It's filling me with fears.
The teacher is talking,
But it sounds like he's squawking.
Hey wait a minute; just look what I've found.
A dancing key lay in front of me!

> The line of words is a star,
> It is shining from afar.
> It's leading me straight to a gate,
> Just inside is my fate.

A swirling cloud of dust, I must, I must, I must.
Like a sword in a man, I thrust my hand into the sand.
To determine what I should put.
Then suddenly . . .

> I've got it, I've got it, I've got it!
> I pulled my hand right out of my pocket,
> Like a plug from a socket.

I put pen to paper and did not waver,
On what I should put, 'twas an instinct from my gut.
It's done, it's done, but what will it get?
I don't know, not yet!

Andrew King (12)
Burscough Priory High School

WWW.(WORLD WIDE WINTERNET)

The thunder in China,
Could never be finer.
But a flash of light,
Can be quite a fright.
Floods in France,
We're all in a trance.
Though they're small,
Cos there's no rain at all!

Tornadoes in Brazil,
Can make you feel quite ill.
So if you see a doctor,
Be sure you do not shock her!
And sleet in Norway,
Can cause you to say
We're all going to get very wet!

All this cold weather,
Which stops almost never,
Can make you feel quite depressed.
So if you want sun,
No more stress,
Lots of fun.
Take a ride on the plane,
To all-sunny Spain!

Gemma Wilkins (13)
Burscough Priory High School

CHOCOLATE

The leaves are green like leaping frogs,
The fruit is brown coffee,
The beans fall as the dancing branches sway.

Swishing around in the factory machines,
Like a river flowing through a valley,
What will be added next?

Gooey caramel-lava in a volcano,
Bumpy nut-mountains towering above me,
Crumbly biscuit-weathered cliffs breaking into the sea.

As I open the silvery wrapper, I smell heaven,
As I bit into its contents I taste heaven,
When I finish I think . . .
Have I been in heaven?

A smooth, brown Galaxy filled with chewy, crunchy, lumpy planets.
The all new delicious dream of a chocolate bar - *a mouthful of space!*

Emma Griggs (12)
Burscough Priory High School

WAR

War is spiteful, mean and cruel
Cold-blooded heartless people
Conflicting hurtful quarrels all the time
Uncontrollable violence makes a bloody mess
Harmful squabbles, scraps and rows
Casualties everywhere no more left to spare
The world is empty
The world is pointless
There is nothing left because of . . . War.

Rebecca Hayton (12)
Burscough Priory High School

STORMY WEATHER

I'm safe in my room
But!
The wind howls like a wolf in the night.
I'm safe in my room
But!
Thunder crashes like a herd of elephants.
I'm safe in my room
But!
Lightning flashes like fireworks in the sky.
I'm safe my room
But!
Rain seeps through the window like tears from a baby.
I'm safe in Mum's room
Asleep.

Adele Leadbetter (12)
Burscough Priory High School

RUGBY

A push and a pull
Fight like a bull
The crowd gives a roar
They want to score four
The saints give a cry
As Wigan score a try
The goal is scored Faz
Gives a shout
The saints are out
The super league is ours.

Lorren Percy (12)
Burscough Priory High School

MY DREAM

I dreamt of my life when I was small, it doesn't seem like
 a dream at all,
I see myself at the age of four, I'm walking towards,
 a large brown door,
I walk inside this room I see, but there's a large man
stood in front of me,
He picks me up and takes me away, I don't want to go,
 I want to stay,
I start to cry, I cry aloud, so then he puts me in a crowd,
A crowd of children quite like me, but some are four and others three,
I crawl towards this girl I see, she says her name is Emily,
We want to get out of this horrible place, so I put on my coat
and she ties her lace,
We crawl towards a large glass door, but Emily stopped,
she crawled no more,
Now a man's walking towards me and shouts 'Here they are look, see,'
I try to get away from them, then I wake up, it's half past ten!

Amy-Jane Hooton (12)
Burscough Priory High School

THE MOON

The moon, have you ever
Looked at it and wondered?
Wondered if it is really
Made of cheese?
I think it's like a big
Balloon, that inflates at
Night and deflates in the day.
Who knows maybe one day
I'll fly into space, stand on
The moon and have a taste.

Lee Walton (12)
Burscough Priory High School

MY HOLIDAY

'Are we there yet?' I ask my mum,
I'm on the aeroplane.
We're on our way to Malta,
I'm not coming home again!

I can't wait to see the sea,
Do you think there'll be much sand?
The island isn't all that big,
There's not even much land!

We're meeting them there aren't we,
By the swimming pool?
I wonder if it's very big?
This will be so cool!

I hope it will be very hot,
Though at the moment there's no sun.
I can't wait to see Sue again,
It's going to be such fun.

Bang! Ouch! That hurt my ears.
Did we just crash or land?
Oh I'm so glad we're here at last!
Let's check out the sea and sand.

I can see them in the pool,
David's splashing Sue!
They're swimming over towards us,
Move or they'll splash you.

I have got everything I could ever want,
Here with me. Oh such bliss.
But saying that, Michael Owen
Wouldn't go a miss!

Lianne Upton (12)
Burscough Priory High School

THE STRANGER

She was walking through the garden
She said that I was strange
She told me she used to live here
I thought she was deranged.

When she had gone away
I went to tell my dad his face went white as snow
I didn't ask him what went wrong
I thought I better not.

I went to town one day
I came with lots of money
I saw the woman that was in my garden
I quickly ran and bought some honey.

I ran back home and hid in bed
Until I heard a knock at the door
I stayed in bed until I thought it had stopped
A few minutes later I heard some more.

I ran downstairs and opened the door
To my surprise it was the stranger
But then I realised
It was my long lost Auntie Granger.

Adam Walsh (12)
Burscough Priory High School

DRAGONS

In the sky a monster lurks
Wings ten times bigger than an eagle's
Eyes as red as Hell
Flames like lava-flow
Wise as a lion
Big as a mountain.

14

Some live in caves
With rotting corpses
Smelling worse than dirty socks.
Dark as the night
And evil as the devil
Guarding pots of gold.

Andrew Rollins (13)
Burscough Priory High School

HAMSTER'S PLAY

Hides away and goes to sleep,
In his little house.
It's only small, a ball of fluff,
No it's not a mouse.

At night he comes out,
Has a drink and eats.
His favourite food is lettuce,
And likes his chocolate treats.

He runs around his cage,
Getting very dizzy.
His name is the name of a plant,
But it's not Bizzie Lizzie.

He goes back to sleep,
When it is light.
He'll come out again,
The very next night.

He's not called Jack,
Harry or Polly.
In fact he is, my hamster Holly.

Heather Doherty (12)
Burscough Priory High School

THE BROKEN PEACE

All is silent: nothing to hear
Still as a tree. Nothing moves.
Although a disaster is near,
Suddenly the ground rocks,
The trees sway violently:
No longer smooth.
The animals run as fast as the wind
With fear and confusion in their minds.
The volcanic eruption has begun.
The mountain roars, before vomiting raw,
Red, radiant lava, fast and unkind.
Spilling down the mountain's body, like a baby,
Drooling its dinner down its front.
Rampaging through the wood, the lava lets nothing
get in its way, like a selfish person pushing through
a crowd.
The traumatised trees twisting and turning,
but burning helplessly.
The animals are as doomed as the trees: their fate creeps up
on them and within seconds, they are no longer loud,
The mountain falls in on itself, and stops the destroying rage,
but the peace will not go on endlessly.

Will Meredith (12)
Burscough Priory High School

MY LIFE AS A CLOWN

Hello my name is Cocoa and I'm a clown
And every time I walk to town,
People laugh at my bright red nose
And my really baggy clothes.

My feet are big and very long
And when I try to sing a song,
People stop to clap their hands
And I have made a lot of fans.

Cathy Chandley (12)
Burscough Priory High School

THE LORD OF AFRICA

His tail was like a waving arm
Stay away or he might cause you harm!
With teeth as white as glistening snow
Here is the Lord of the animal kingdom lying low!

Eyes as bright as the sun
A roar like the blast of a gun
Golden fur like a field of corn
Here is a menacing lion, I could have sworn!

Roaming Africa, wild and free
Looking for his lunch, what can he see?
Grazing gazelles inching along
A charming blue bird singing a heavenly song.

Grey rocks that stood in a crowd
Sad, old people that are not loud
Dotted trees like a silent army
And seeing for the first time, a lioness looking smarmy!

Racing over, the large lion saw
A tiny lion cub with a wound in his paw
Licking the cut with his kingly charm
Africa is safe it will come to no harm.

Pamela Dee (12)
Burscough Priory High School

TIGERS

I love tigers of any kind,
Small or large - I don't mind,
I love tigers roaming free,
Not under lock and key.

I love tigers for their eyes,
Like an owl's knowing and wise,
I love tigers for their coats,
Smooth and silky like a stoats.

I love tigers but not their teeth,
Cunning and evil in my belief,
I love tigers but not their roar,
It trembles the earth and makes my ears sore.

I love tigers and watching them play,
Swimming and climbing all the day,
I love tigers for their stripes, which are lovely and unique,
As they creep and crawl and crouch, it makes them hard to seek.

Jessica MacRae (12)
Burscough Priory High School

THE LION

The lion was creeping through the grass,
Then all of a sudden there was a big crash.

A big oak tree came crashing down,
This knocked off the lion's crown.

Away he ran down through the trees,
With cuts and bruises to his knees.

Blood came pouring down from his head,
Then he slowly made it to his bed.

His lady friend a wise old snake,
Brought him some meat on a plate.

When she arrived at his gate,
She couldn't believe the state
Of her greatest mate.

Ashley Robinson (13)
Burscough Priory High School

GORILLA

Gorilla's hair is like a wire brush
He sits on his little tusch.
Fur like a cat pitch black.
Hands rubbery and fat
No one notices that he's rather fat.
Like a rolled up mat
He swings through the trees while
Scratching his fleas
And ending up on his knees.
Eating the bees
He thinks they're leaves,
Late at night
The stars are bright
He feels a fright
Who is it lurking in the night?
The birds take flight,
Oh what a sight!
The sun rises,
Now everything is right.

Kelly Rix (12)
Burscough Priory High School

MY RAINBOW

Red
A red stripe to start my rainbow off.
As red as a rose.
It is as bright and red as Rudolf's nose.

Orange
An orange stripe to follow.
As orange as a marigold.
The colour stands out bright and bold.

Yellow
A yellow band in the sky.
The buttercup reflection.
Is like pastry on an apple pie.

Green
A green blade of grass.
Is a cricket's wing.
It's ever so satisfying, it's fit for a king.

Blue
A ribbon of blue like the deep deep sea.
It fills me full of joyful glee.
I jump and hop like a dancing flea.

Indigo
This is one of my favourite colours.
It's full of mystery, it gives me the shudders.
When I think of this wonderful shade.
It makes me think of my garden spade.

Violet
A damson has fallen to the ground.
It's landed on a black mole mound.
But even this soft spongy landing.
The damson has popped and started oozing.

Emma Frankland (12)
Burscough Priory High School

NO FUEL

Pumps are empty there's no fuel
Walking everywhere, that's so cruel!
No chance to play the game I like
Can't fit a snooker cue on my bike.

Cars stand idle, lorries too
How will police and ambulances get through?
Roads deserted no traffic about
It's getting serious there's no doubt.

Mum and Dad can't get to work
We're under siege it's like Dunkirk,
How will I be getting to school?
Stay at home, that would be cool.

On my PlayStation watching telly
Eating, drinking, food in my belly,
But soon there'll be no food to buy
When supermarket shelves run dry.

Our petrol tanks as dry as bones
Like singers without microphones.
So let's get together and end this mess
Tony Blair please hear my SOS.

Daniel Jassi (12)
Burscough Priory High School

DON'T ASK STUPID QUESTIONS

'Mum, how do we breathe?'
'Don't ask stupid questions.'
'Mum, why do I have to go to school?'
'Don't ask stupid questions.'
'Mum, why do I have a brother?'
'Don't ask stupid questions.'

'Fine, I won't ask questions.'
'I didn't say that you couldn't ask questions,
I said, don't ask stupid questions.'

'Dad, why am I alive?'
'Don't ask stupid questions.'
'Dad, why don't you let Mum drive?'
'Don't ask stupid questions.'
'Dad, how old are you?'
'Don't ask stupid questions.'

'Fine, I won't ask questions.'
'I didn't say that you couldn't ask questions,
I said, don't ask stupid questions.'

Rhiannon Williams (12)
Burscough Priory High School

SPACE

The stars twinkle like sparkling diamonds in the sky
The big planets are the shape of oranges
The space is dark like my basement
The shooting stars fly through the dark night
The planets are spectacular like the rainbow
The shuttle shakes like a shaker.

Chris Forshaw (12)
Burscough Priory High School

WOOF! WOOF!

Woof! Woof! Goes my dog at night,
Woof! Woof! Something's in her sight.

Woof! Woof! I hope she's alright,
Woof! Woof! I'm going down to see her.

Woof! Woof! It's only a fright,
Woof! Woof! There's a man far out of sight.

Woof! Woof! The man's like a stranger in the night,
Woof! Woof! The man's gone now far, far away.

Woof! Woof! My dog's as proud as a peacock,
Woof! Woof! My dog's fast asleep.

Woof! Woof!

Liam Waite (12)
Burscough Priory High School

THE CHALLENGE

The boy looked upward from his bike,
The road unfolded before him like a coiled serpent,
He had never taken this route before
And he wondered whether his ability would match the gradient,
As he began his journey up the serpent.
His heart was a drum beating rapidly,
His legs moved as pistons pumping him further,
Climbing with every revolution,
His legs screamed inwardly for more fuel,
His mouth gaped to accept more air,
His chest expanding and contracting like a balloon,
Pumping energy and life round his body.

Matthew Marsland (13)
Burscough Priory High School

THE BOX

There was a box,
A cardboard box on a windy hill.
In that box there is a cloud,
So big and round like an elephant.

There was a box,
A cardboard box on a windy hill.
Now that box blew away,
It's gone on its terrible way.

There was a box,
A cardboard box on a windy hill.
Now it's gone there's nothing left,
But a grey cloud on a windy hill.

Robert Ashcroft (12)
Burscough Priory High School

MY DOG

My dog he likes his walks,
He sometimes tries to talk.
But when I'm not home from school
He sits upstairs acting cool.

But when I come home from school,
He knocks me over like a feather.
But that's OK it didn't hurt
Because my carpet's soft like feathers.

When I go to bed at night,
He jumps upon my bed.
But as I get up on a morning,
He's still there resting like the dead.

Gemma Ashcroft (12)
Burscough Priory High School

GETTING CLOSER

What's that over there?
Oh it's just my mind, I don't care.
But wait something's moving,
Lurching in the shadows,
Getting closer and closer to me.

As it moves, it kinda grooves,
To the music I have on.
It creeps about,
Like it has lost its way,
Like an eagle waiting to catch its prey,
And every minute it's getting closer to me.

Oh wait, I can see its hands,
No fingers, just shaped like frying pans.
I bet you it's been to lots of different lands,
Gobbling lots of people, even whole bands,
and it is now very close and getting even closer to me.

Lucy Edwards (12)
Burscough Priory High School

MMMM CHOCOLATE!

C   hocolics love
H   eaps and heaps of it
O   odles of it
C   onstantly
O   ooh lovely
L   ots of it
A   ll the
T   ime
E   very day.

Kester Cranfield (13)
Burscough Priory High School

THE DRAGON

Red hot like a poker its tongue on fire
Its bright blue eyes shining like sapphires
Small mean and arrogant on a magnificent head
When I look into its eyes it's a wonder I'm not dead.

Its claws like talons its tail like a knife,
I am wondering now just how long is my life?
With a flash of gold and the crack of a gun
Another dragon soared round my head, I wanted to run.

I started to move it follows me,
Its wings are surrounding I cannot see
It swoops down alone, this is the end
And then I see all it wants is a friend.

I can see its eyes brimming with tears
How stupid I was, what is there to fear?
It takes a step closer I'm still not sure,
Whilst I hesitate it lets out a mighty roar.
The whole cave shook with its frustration and rage
What should I do I'm trapped in a cage.

It spread its wings and took to the sky
Where will it go how long can it fly?
Sadness and remorse now came to me
He wasn't a bad dragon was he?

I walked sadly along the desert, alone along the land
Keeping hope that I should hear his wings across the sand
And ever since that day the friendly dragon came
I have never been able to keep away the feeling of sad shame.

Sally Evans (12)
Burscough Priory High School

SPIDER

Spider hanging from a line
Suspended above the world
Created a long thin twine
The long thin line becoming swirled.

When the web is finished
the waiting game begins
It turns out very glinted
Time to pray to release.

When the unexpected fly appears
The spider waits . . . *bang*
The fly's more scared than his biggest fears
The spider scares it with his fang.

Struggle, struggle but no escape
The terrorist has his hostage tied
The spider manhandles the fly as though it were an ape
The spider sighs in relief.

All of that work on the web destroyed
All that is left to do is to eat
But surely you would be annoyed
So that work and no mess very neat.

At winter where do you go
In the nearest house
Come in, come in you might be seen, don't be slow
Beware watch out for that mouse.

Oh no you've been seen
Run, hide, your life is nearly fulfilled
Please don't kill me I hear you scream
Killed!

Adrian Smith (12)
Burscough Priory High School

THE TRACTOR

Tractor oh tractor
Going so slow,
Will you hurry
So then I can go.

Tractor oh tractor
Working so hard,
Don't break now
You're far from the yard.

Tractor oh tractor
Will you hurry,
I don't want to be
Late for my curry.

Richard Seddon (12)
Burscough Priory High School

GONNA POUNCE

Rustling around in the tall green grass,
Ready to pounce on prey that'll pass.

Moving a step closer,
Widening her eyes,
Ready to give her prey,
One heck of a big surprise.

Taking a step forward as quiet as can be,
Gonna jump out any minute now,
Just you wait and see.

Lauren Halton (12)
Burscough Priory High School

SPIDERS

A spider is a revolting insect,
The one thing I hate in life.
All they do is sit there
Waiting to give me a fright.

They have legs that look like twigs,
And eyes that sit on stalks.
It makes me feel quite funny
When they creep across the floor.

In the bath they like to be,
Or hanging from their webs.
But worst of all I hate them
To be crawling on my bed.

Lindsey Houghton (12)
Burscough Priory High School

MY BROTHER PETER

H e is horrible to me
A ttacks me
T ickles me
E ats my sweets.

A nnoys me
N ever nags much
D eserves praise

L ooks after me
O ften helps me with golf
V ery kind sometimes
E ncourages me.

Tim Kennedy (12)
Burscough Priory High School

My Cat

Fighty - bitey
Proud - mighty,
Skulking - sulking
Moonlight - cat.

Fence - clawing
Tree - sawing,
Ground - pawing
Midnight - cat.

Choir - singing
Ear - ringing,
Present - bringing
Nightsight - cat.

Lap - curling
Loud - purring,
Curtain - tearing
My - cat.

Jesika MacGuire (12)
Burscough Priory High School

My Fat Dog

I had a dog who was very fat,
The basket was where he always sat,
He sometimes sat on the mat like a cat.
When I said walkies he would sit
Down and frown.
He ate too much and exploded
R I P
To my poor dog who was too
Overloaded!

Charlotte Monaghan (12)
Burscough Priory High School

THIS GIRL IN MY CLASS

I have this girl in my class,
She isn't very tall.
She never stops talking,
She drives me up the wall.

Her hair is short,
Rather like her body.
Her eyes are brown,
Just like a little doggy.

She sits next to me in most lessons,
She drives me round the bend.
Her voice makes me go crazy,
One day I hope, it will all end.

I like her really, really I do,
But if you met her,
I'm sure you'd like her too!

Samantha Davies (12)
Burscough Priory High School

THE BIRD BY THE LAKE

Gliding through the air
Like a swan upon a lake,
Gracefully swooping down to catch
A fish in the lake.

Flying through the valley
Like a road towards the lake,
Watching the people as they walk
While he just sits by the lake.

Andrew O'Brien (13)
Burscough Priory High School

MY MUM

My mum's from out of space,
I daren't let anyone know,
She drinks toothpaste
And eats fine lace,
But I daren't let anyone know.

She doesn't have a job,
Her species is flolabob,
She bites her nails
And has five tails,
I daren't let anyone know.

She runs like a cheetah,
Her husband's name is Peter,
She has purple eyes,
Her hair is full of flies,
I daren't let anyone know.

I don't care if she's an alien,
She still has a mother's touch,
I don't care what anyone says,
I love her very much.

Rebecca Sarbutts (12)
Burscough Priory High School

THE DOVE

I have a dove, a white soft dove,
She means peace and is never overlooked,
She is graceful and works hard,
She means no harm to all creatures.

I call her Mum.

Scott Bradley (12)
Burscough Priory High School

THE LORD OF THE JUNGLE

The tiger is lord of the jungle,
The one that I know is called Phil.
All other beasties are humble,
Except for a lion called Bill.

Now Bill is a lion of virtue,
That no other cat can deny,
Phil it said wouldn't hurt you,
Bill's got sharp claws and an evil red eye.

One day while Phil was out walking,
He met Gladys a tiger of pride,
Phil was never a cat much for stalking,
Except when Bill's at her side.

Then Bill turned his eyes on the stalker,
While Philip of course he thought 'Cripes'
But he still had ambitions to walk her,
So that's why the tiger has 'stripes.'

Emma O'Brien (12)
Burscough Priory High School

THE HYENA

I have a hyena,
He laughs a lot but when he's mad
He's angry!
When he shouts it makes me cry.
He's not a fox, he is not sly.
He lives in the loft
I call him Dad.

Joel Cornah (13)
Burscough Priory High School

SAW

I saw a gnome doing a dance
And a man with ants in his pants,
I also saw a dog walking in the air,
With a boy balancing on a chair,
There was a girl with curls,
With a tortoise doing twirls.

I saw a chimpanzee doing a play,
I thought I saw a boy made of clay
And there was a cat barking,
With a fish charping,
I also saw a king in a pie
And a pillow 6 feet high.

I also saw a television walking
And a clock talking
With a lamp eating
And a printer reading,
Unfortunately that was all I saw in one day,
But whatever you do don't ever say,
It's impossible because it's not,
Just use your imagination to think up a word
And you will soon like what you have heard.

Emma Culshaw (13)
Burscough Priory High School

THE LION

I have a lion, a hairy lion
He's very loud and snores at night,
His face is rough and whiskery,
I call him Dad.

Darren Jones (12)
Burscough Priory High School

ENGLAND! ENGLAND!

Flag bearers are marching at the front
Behind us plays the band
We are all soldiers of fortune
And we are shouting for England.
We are going to march
Till we reach the battleground
Feel the tense atmosphere
And hear the surround sound.
We scare the opposition
By singing a war song
We all stand united
We know our side is strong.
We are looking for a victory
And it can be done
It just needs luck and courage
For this thing to be won.
This may all sound to you like war
And this excuse may be a bit tame
But the fact of the matter is
We are all going to a football game!

Stuart Garrett (12)
Burscough Priory High School

MY SOFT RABBIT

I have a rabbit, a soft,
Smooth rabbit.
I love her so much,
She is hard working
And lovely.
I call her Mum.

Sarah Spencer (12)
Burscough Priory High School

UNDER THE SEA

Under the sea
There are wonderful creatures,
So amazing to me
With all of their features.

Dolphins, whales and the seahorse,
Lobsters, crabs
And starfish of course.

I would love to explore the sea.
To see its wonders
Just my friend and me.

Off to Australia we would go
To the Great Barrier Reef
Where the fish glow.

What an adventure that would be
A chance of a lifetime
Just my friend and me.

Kathryn Pell (12)
Burscough Priory High School

MY FLOWERS

My flowers have many powers,
The power to grow,
The power to overcome the snow.

It has come to autumn
The leaves fall
And the cold wind terrorises all.

And now my flowers have gone to bed,
I will keep them warm in the garden shed
And when summer comes round again
And there is not more cold winter rain.

My flowers will bloom once again.

Emma Skinner (12)
Burscough Priory High School

MY PLAYSTATION

My PlayStation is so cool,
But the bad thing is I can't play it at school.

My PlayStation is so great,
I play it at least till half-past eight.

My PlayStation is so good,
It's better than playing in lots of mud.

My PlayStation is so fine,
It's better than swinging on a vine.

My PlayStation is so splendid,
It's never needed to be mended.

My PlayStation totally rocks,
It's better than smelly socks.

My PlayStation is not bad,
But sometimes it makes me mad.

My PlayStation is the best,
It's better than all the rest.

Oliver Rushworth (12)
Burscough Priory High School

THE STORMY SEA

Bang! Crash!
Whooosh!
Is what the stormy sea does
Over the hills and into the sea
The stormy sea has risen,
Into the night and into the day
The stormy sea is still there
The fog has cleared
But the glare's still there
In the distance you can see
What seems to be a party,
Not on an island not on a
Ship, but it's on the other side,
Of what seems to be it.

Sarah Hesketh (12)
Burscough Priory High School

TREES

A tree is like you or me,
The only thing is they can't speak or see.

The leaves are like the palm of your hand,
Some light, some dark throughout the land.

The bark is like your body skin,
It shows its age and grows within.

Like you and I the trees it dies
And never again will it be alive.

Laura Hussey (12)
Burscough Priory High School

THE TRAIN

The train was moving as fast as lightning,
The noise was furious and very frightening.
The train was as blue as the sea
As it came towards me.
I get a chill down my spine
When they come time after time
It's like a long snake
Make no mistake
About its sound
It sounds like it's going tac-a-tick tac
As it slides down the track
It's gone past
Really fast
Goodbye
Train!

James McDonald (12)
Burscough Priory High School

LIFE

Life is like a bee,
Buzzing all day,
Looking for its prey.

Life is as long as
A ball of string,
It keeps getting longer!

Life is like one big gobstopper,
With all the different colours,
But which one is coming next?

Katie Dawson (12)
Burscough Priory High School

My House Is A Zoo

My house is a zoo
My brother is like a kangaroo
He hops and jumps
And likes to eat Flumps.

My house is a zoo
My mum is like a gnu
She bounces and bangs
And likes to eat meringues.

My house is a zoo
The noise that we make is a hullabaloo
There isn't much chance for you to snore
But my zoo house is never a bore!

Rebecca Flynn (12)
Burscough Priory High School

My Nan

My nan is a lovely lady,
Who's very large and plump,
When she walks across the floorboards,
You hear the room go bump.

She has a sense of humour,
Her cheeks blow in and out
And when she laughs too hard,
Her false teeth fall out.

She might be getting old and grey
But we never worry,
She manages to get around
But never in a hurry.

Hayley Rooney (12)
Burscough Priory High School

MR TOWLER'S DOG PEE WEE

Mr Towler next door to me,
Has a dog called Pee Wee,
He barks, he growls, he breaks everything,
But Mr Towler treats him like a king.

He is golden like the sun
And he weighs a ton,
He is as tall as a horse
And smells like tomato sauce.

My mum really likes him
And so does my friend,
But I hate that dog
And the noise will never end.

Faye Singleton (12)
Burscough Priory High School

MY HIPPOPOTAMUS

I have a hippopotamus,
He's big and fat and fun.
His eyes are like huge diamonds,
They glisten in the sun.

I keep him in my bedroom
And feed him on French peas.
He's like a little elephant,
He washes with such ease.

He sleeps inside the bathtub,
He drinks expensive wine.
He eats while standing on his head,
But best of all he's mine!

Lawrence Rhodes (12)
Burscough Priory High School

MONSTERS OF THE NIGHT

A hand of claws from under my bed,
A slimy arm grabs at my head,
A ghoulish moan like a haunting ghost,
A rattle like chains from behind my bed post,
A creature with teeth like sharpened knives,
It bares its claws and its piercing eyes,
A tentacle all slimy and gross,
I felt a presence coming close,
A luke warm breath meets my face,
My heart is beating like in a race,
I close my eyes shut them tight,
I hold the covers with all my might,
The creature now is at my side,
That very moment I want to cry.

James Joyce (12)
Burscough Priory High School

MY PET DOLPHIN

I have a pet dolphin, he lives in the sea,
We have a special bond, yes him and me.
I go to see him every day,
After school at Whitby bay.

I treat him like my little toy,
Not to mention my favourite boy.
He's as cute as a teddy bear,
The kind that you win at the fair.

I bring him sweets and treats galore,
As each day, I love him more.
His skin is as blue as the sea,
What a lovely colour to be.

My name for him is Bubble,
As he causes me a lot of trouble.
No, I love him dearly
Cos he's my best friend really.

Natalie Beesley (12)
Burscough Priory High School

IRENE

Irene is as thin as a goal post,
She is as blonde as the sunshine,
She has eyes as blue as the sky.

Irene likes to work very hard,
She works her fingers to the bone,
She likes to rest every now and then
And watch her favourite programme.
She'd put her feet up and stay there all day,
Now when the resting time is done,
She's start all over again.

Now Irene's friends from where she lives,
Would say, 'Oh what a lovely garden you have got.'
You work so hard every single day,
Make sure you take a rest.
She thanked them very much,
Then worked the day away.

Jonathan William Haynes (12)
Burscough Priory High School

THE FOOTBALLER

One of an army of eleven men
He plays in a dream team with stars galore
A goal hungry player who's fast and fit
Out shining other players
With his dazzling kit.

He glides down the wing
With the rush of the wind
Dribbling and passing with the greatest of ease
He heads the ball forward
And curls the corner in.

Making for the goal mouth he's nearly made his trip
Penalty he cries as he's fouled and hits the deck
Now the tension's rising
The ball is on the spot
He's about to score the one he almost never got.

Martin Cliffe (12)
Burscough Priory High School

DREAMS

I lie in bed dreaming,
Just dreaming the night away.
When I wake up to go to school,
I wish that I could stay.

Incredible things can happen in dreams,
You can fly up to the stars,
Or save the world from a monster,
With eyes as red as Mars.

You can turn your teachers into frogs,
Go swimming in chocolate ice-cream,
You can do anything
Because it is your dream.

But sometimes you get a nightmare
And it's really, really bad,
When you wake up from it,
You're actually quite glad.

Lauren Claire Fairley (12)
Burscough Priory High School

GROWING UP

At the age of 1, I could shout,
By the age of 2, I could tie a shoe,
When I came to 3, I could kneel on one knee

At the age of 4, I could answer the door,
When I came to 5, I could sprint and dive,
At the age of 6, I could dance and twist,
At the age of 7, I could look up to heaven,
When I came to 8, I looked up to fate.

By the age of 9, I could draw and rhyme,
When I came to 10, I could spell like a gem,
At the age of 11, I studied heaven,
At the age of 12, I could do primes and factors,
By the age of 13, I began to grow
And by the age of 14 . . . well I'd like to know.

Daniel Smith (12)
Burscough Priory High School

THE FOX POEM

I am as red as fire,
I am as sly as a wolf,
I am as furry as a mink,
I am as fast as a hare.

I come out at night,
I kill more than I eat,
My tail is like a brush,
My eyes glow like Christmas lights.

I care for my young,
I seem cruel,
I am cunning,
I am also cute as a hamster.

My teeth are as sharp as daggers,
My claws are like nails,
My ears are like bat ears,
My nose is like a dog's nose.

Terry Moore (12)
Burscough Priory High School

MY DOG

My dog isn't from a common breed
And he's quiet and reserved,
But when it comes to meal times,
He's really quite a rogue.

He eats his breakfast for his tea,
As though it's as normal as can be
And though he doesn't eat a lot,
He really is rather fat.

He's as lazy as a tortoise,
But perhaps not quite as slow,
In fact he can run incredibly fast,
But no one would ever know.

He's got grey lines around his eyes
And one going down his nose,
To say he's old would be telling lies,
He's young and lazy I suppose.

Amanda Griffiths (12)
Burscough Priory High School

MY DREAM

Oh how one day I'd love to be the best
And to rise above the rest.
To jump as high into the sky as a soaring
Bird that starts to fly.

This dream I have is on my bike
And on the days that I would be the
Best to beat.

I have thought what I might be
What my future life may be?
Will I be famous or will I not?
A life full of adventure at home
Or at sea?

Life as a rugby player or life as a builder,
When the day comes that I must choose,
I may be famous or I may not.
But as long as I'm happy then that's all I'll be.

Christopher Slinger (12)
Burscough Priory High School

SPOOKY HOUSE

There's a spooky house down my lane
It is beginning to be quite a pain
I'm scared to go by
In case I suddenly die.

There's a bird on its roof that looks at me
But when I walk past it begins to flee
I don't know where it goes, I don't really care,
But I know for certain, I want to get out of there.

I don't want to go near
Because of all my built up fear
I'm as scared as an elephant to a mouse
I don't want to go near that spooky house.

Kristian Marr (12)
Burscough Priory High School

A MUSIC POEM

This poem is to help you remember
What types of music there are,
From pop to rock, country to classic
And heavy metal if you go that far.

Soul is said to be the food of life
And blues the sad melody,
Classic is like opera and such,
But my favourite is R 'n' B.

Life is written in the country song
And how you feel in pop,
Garage is one you can dance to
As well as hip-hop.

Jennifer Crampton (13)
Burscough Priory High School

BIG CATS

Prowling, scheming,
Growling, roar!
Hiding behind,
An open jaw.

Stripes 'n' spots,
Plain 'n' black,
Sharp and pointed,
Teeth in a stack.

Seeing the next,
Unlucky victim,
Circling stealthily.
Stalking him.

Waiting until the
Time is right,
Then going in,
For the fatal bite!

Sarah Scarisbrick (12)
Burscough Priory High School

MY RABBIT

My rabbit is like a cuddly toy,
His name is Pie and he's a boy,
He's fat and fluffy and full of fun,
You should see him in his run,
He jumps about and flicks his feet
And sometimes escapes onto the street,
His ears point up to the sky,
I think you'd like my rabbit - Pie.

Iain Stephenson (12)
Burscough Priory High School

JUST AN ORDINARY WALK

Just an ordinary walk,
Upon the cliffs of chalk,
When an ordinary rock,
Fell into my sock.

Just an ordinary walk,
With quite a lot of talk,
When an ordinary cat,
Fell off the cliff and splat!

Just an ordinary walk,
Well, except for the hawk,
When an ordinary clown,
Nearly made the hawk frown.

Just an ordinary walk,
When we heard the pop of a cork,
When an ordinary poem,
Ended with the characters going!

Michael Gray (12)
Burscough Priory High School

SYDNEY 2000

The girls and boys play basketball
Most of them are really tall
When she's running like a cheetah,
I'm sure she's going to beat her,
Well, I'm sure glad it's not me,
Cos I'm only watching it on the TV!

Gemma Watson (12)
Burscough Priory High School

I REALLY MUSTN'T GROW TOO TALL

I'm going to have an attic room,
Of my own very soon,
Dad is working night and day,
To make it perfect in every way.

I'm going to have an attic room,
Of my own very soon,
I'm very excited about it all,
I really mustn't grow too tall.

I'm going to have an attic room,
Of my own very soon,
We're going to paint it very pale blue
With lots of white fluffy clouds too.

I'm going to have an attic room,
Of my own very soon,
I'm very excited I can't contain myself.

Benjamin McLoughlin (12)
Burscough Priory High School

MY HENS

My hens are like small, clucking dinosaurs,
They are soft and cuddly like a well used pillow.
The two small birds have sharp beaks and claws,
They work even better than axes and saws.
Their combs are red, as red as blood,
But for their baths, they use the mud.

Richard Whitney (12)
Burscough Priory High School

DAY AND NIGHT

The stars twinkle as bright as light,
They are my guides throughout the night.

The moon shines as bright as day,
I look and stare, but it never fades away.

The sun glows as brightly as fire,
Day after day, it gets higher and higher.

The dew on the lawn is as cold as snow
And it drips in between and of every toe.

The rainbow sparkles as all the colours shine
And has not yet changed since the beginning of time!

Naomi Seddon (13)
Burscough Priory High School

MY BIKE

My bike is as shiny as brass,
As clean as a dish,
As tall as a tree
And as fast as a fish.

The brakes on my bike,
Are as sharp as a knife,
As quick as a cheetah,
I've used them for part of my life.

The colour of my bike,
Is as black as the dark night
And the lights on my bike,
Are very, very bright.

Mark Bailey (12)
Burscough Priory High School

CAT POEM

My cat is like a roaring lion
It wanders round the streets at night.

When it comes in, it is as cool as a cucumber,
As it thinks it rules the house.

It's as fast as a cheetah and eats like a hippo,
It's got ears like a bat
And legs as short as a terrier.

It's fur is soft like a pillow and it is stripy like a tiger,
It hunts like the rest of its family,
Pouncing on things a lot smaller than it.

It tears its prey apart like the lion on a zebra,
At night it sleeps like a koala bear and doesn't get up,
Until it's hungry - roar!

John Martin (13)
Burscough Priory High School

BUMP IN THE NIGHT!

Have you ever wondered what scares you at night?
Something creeping under your bedclothes to give you a fright,
Have you heard the creaking in the carpet
That sends a chill straight up your spine?
And can you hear the ghostly whine
Have you ever heard the wind hit your window at night?
For these are the things that will give you a fright,
These are the things that go bump in the night.

Robert Kenny (12)
Burscough Priory High School

A RAINY DAY

Thunder and lightning clouds drawing in,
People around me are scurrying in,
It's from the rain they want to hide,
As the children rush inside.

Bikes and blades, bats and balls,
'Put them away' is what mum calls,
The thunder echoes all around,
Then lightning brightens up the ground.

The streets are all empty,
There's no one about,
Even the spiders down the spout.

The rain runs down the window and little rivers form,
I am glad I'm on the inside where it's nice and warm,
Drip, drop, drip, down comes the rain,
Crash, bang, wallop that's the thunder again.

The clouds are looking brighter in the distant sky,
Can we go back out to play?
You hear the children cry,
'Yes' says Mum, 'go out and play.'

'Put on your wellies and your macs,
Then into the puddles you may splash.'
'Hip, hip, hooray' the children say
What a great end to a wet and rainy day.

Hannah Hayman (12)
Burscough Priory High School

THE START OF A NEW DAY

The alarm clock is still bleeping
I know it is time to stop sleeping,
Stretching and yawning in my bed
I contemplate the day ahead.

The bathroom is so cold
The warm water will not scold,
Rubbing the towel over my body
It really starts to refresh me.

Look in the mirror to see if I'm OK,
I am still wishing in bed I lay,
Cleaning my glasses on my sweater
They are starting to look a little better.

The kettle turns itself off after boiling,
As I am at the table with my cereal eating,
Over to the fridge to fetch the milk jug
To pour onto the tea in my mug.

Tying my shoe laces in a knot
And grabbing the bag which I haven't forgot,
Opening the door 'Goodbye' I said
Still contemplating the day ahead.

Charlie Bunting (12)
Burscough Priory High School

SHEEP IN MY GARDEN

I've got a sheep in my garden,
She's as woolly as a cloud.
I love her most of the time
But not when she's loud.

She stands there like a lemon,
She is a great big teddy bear.
All big and cuddly,
Waiting for a child's care.

I feed her bread, carrots too,
Nearly break a nail or two,
But when she eats your clothes,
You wish they were not new.

The bad thing about my sheep,
Is when she eats the plants,
My whole family say,
She's like a herd of ants.

My sheep is like an elephant,
When she wants to be fed.
But best of all,
Is when she rests her little head.

Sarah Potter (12)
Burscough Priory High School

ANIMALS

Animals come in all different shapes and sizes
From cheetahs very rough to lions extremely tough.

Lizards as green as leaves on a summer tree
A trail of tiny ants as far as you can see.

A school of little yellow fish as bright as the sun
Chimps very cheeky having lots of fun.

From coloured fish all shiny and bright
To a swimming seal streamlined and light.

Megan Brocken (13)
Burscough Priory High School

I'M GOING HOME!

Darkness hovers like a hawk over its prey,
The moon shines as brightly as a torch down
A misty lane,
The ferocious wind howls like a hungry wolf,
Shouts of 'Batten down your hatches!'
As the noisy rain pours in triumph!

'Pitter-patter, pitter-patter,' louder gets the rain,
Like a big brass band the hail begins to pain.
The rain upon my bare face, whips coldly
Like a whirlwind.
My cheeks sting red like a stinging nettle
Wrapped tightly round and pulling.

I'm still at the bus stop late at night like a statue in the fog,
After waiting, waiting . . . waiting at last a glimmer of hope,
The bus arrives like a surge of comfort,
The doors fling open wide,
Like a welcoming hand the warm air hits me,
I smile with comfort inside.

Thoughts turn to pleasure as my snug duvet
Beckons me home,
A good feeling of warmth and comfort and a
Mug of Mum's piping hot tea!

Charlotte Binns (12)
Burscough Priory High School

SUNSET

The end of a beautiful day
Sit far away from the noise
On high mountain tops and
Watch the sun go down.
It made the glorious day shine bright
Beautiful colours in the sky
Purple, pink and red.
Sun go down behind the sea
Reflections on the waves
Watch very slowly as it goes down.
It disappears, night has come
With the moon and stars
Time for a wonderful night
It is ours.

Samantha Fairclough (12)
Glenburn High School

THE STAR FAIRY

Quicker than the speed of lightning
Don't be scared, she's not that frightening,
Softer than a daisy,
Never slow and never lazy
As she dances up in space
Putting on her dress of lace
Watching from up very high
She looks down quiet and shy
Like a rainbow she'll never end
But she'll be there as your friend.

Jamie-Leigh Hardwick (12)
Glenburn High School

WORLD WAR II POEM!

Blimmin' women working all day
Working and working but don't get their pay.

Sent for the war lots of people cried
There was only about 50 per cent that survived
All the rest died.

Everything was dull absolutely nothing bright
Only bombs and air-raids in sight.

Adolf Hitler mad and bad
If someone never tried he'd say you bad old lad.

Children starved nothing to eat
Hitler said come on Germany don't defeat.

If people died this is what the children would say:
I wish, I wish the war would go away.

All people think the war is bad
And because of Hitler suffered and were sad.

This is a poem about World War II
So be careful next time it could be you!

Shana Greer (12)
Glenburn High School

SCHOOL

Packed school bag
Bursting with equipment
All homework done
Brain full to learn.

No teachers!

Stephanie Bradshaw (13)
Glenburn High School

THAT BOY!

That boy he makes me go weak at the knees,
That glint in his eye so shiny,
Those teeth behind those lips,
That boy.

He is the Prince and I the Princess,
The King and me the Queen,
His voice, it makes me quiver,
That boy.

I dream that we are going out,
Going to the movies,
I fancy him like no one else,
That boy.

He doesn't know I love him,
And I don't want him to know,
I'd rather he thought we were just friends,
So I could fantasise about,
That boy.

Toni McCann (11)
Glenburn High School

PLAYSTATION

Control pads in
Joystick ready
Power on
Ready to go . . .
No game!

Chris Berkley (13)
Glenburn High School

DAVE MIRRA BMX

D iving over puddles
A iming for a trick
V ersatile at every skill
E ffort needed for jumps

M ad mongooses
I n all competitions
R amps as high as the sky
R ampworks fun as anything
A mazing tricks to try

B omkers is good
M otorbikes fly
X erosser jumps are too big for bikes.

Anthony Williams (13)
Glenburn High School

PARTY TIME

Wolly the worm went out to play
He came back the very next day
With ice-cream and jelly and lots of
drinks too.
We're having a party for our friend Sue
I've brought lots of decorations
They're all brand new.
Quick everyone hide, here comes Sue
On the count of three
1, 2, 3, *surprise!*

Amanda Smaje (12)
Glenburn High School

HATE

Hate is dark grey
It tastes like sour milk
It smells like sewage
It looks like a deserted town
It sounds like shouting and crying
It feels like sadness, fear, depression.

Samantha Iredale (12)
Glenburn High School

MY DAD

My dad is always late
The one thing about him I hate
But the rest is fun
We laugh a tonne
When I'm with my dad.

Katie McArdle (12)
Glenburn High School

LOVE

Love is a dark red strawberry
It tastes like sweets
It smells like pink blooming roses
It looks like a cute little puppy
It sounds like chirping birds
It makes me feel . . . Special.

Leigh Brady Simpkin
Glenburn High School

You

You,
Your head is like a pizza
You,
Your eyes are like tigers
You,
Your mouth is like a letter box
You,
Your hair is like a brush
You,
Your ears are like a tail
You,
Your body is like a filing cabinet
You
Your legs are like tree trunks
You,
Your feet are like toffees
You,
Your arms are long and stiff
You,
Your hands are like stick insects
You,
I don't like you because you're ugly.

Rebecca Mount (12)
Glenburn High School

Cherry

Small and plump,
Shiny, soft, squashy
Slithers along my tongue
A present from Heaven.

Leanne Hornsby (13)
Glenburn High School

EVERTON

E verton are the best!
V ery close to beating the rest
E nergetic good on the ball
R unning toward the goal it's a fine bet
T he ball is in the back of the net
O ver the season they've done their best
N early as good as the rest.

Philippa Bernard (12)
Glenburn High School

NIGHT PREY

Lurking in the midnight forest
Sneaking slowly in the night
Searching, searching for prey
There it is!
There, pouncing, pouncing, death.

Karl Rowlands (13)
Glenburn High School

MY SISTER

S he is called Amelia and is four years old, and
I n May she'll be five
S he is funny and easy to get on with, but at
T imes she can be a pain
E verytime she makes me laugh
R ather like a hyena.

Jason Wilde (11)
Glenburn High School

MY CATS

I have three black and white cats,
Mitsy, Bow and Domino.
They are all spotty, dotty and wild,
Their spots black as soot, their fur white as snow.
They spit when they are angry,
When they are happy they purr.
They like to sleep in the sunshine,
And clean their soft fur.
They hear things before I do,
They stare at nothing at all,
The dust specks that are drifting,
The fly on the wall.
I love them all dearly,
They are my special cats,
The only thing I don't like about them is
They bring in dead rats!

Donna Tilley (12)
Glenburn High School

MY BROTHER

My mother made my brother
With half a tonne of mud
Twelve million snails and twelve million slugs.

My mother made my brother
With so much pain
But with no brain.

My mother made my brother
With a tube of worms
And too many germs.

Stevi-Lea Denton (12)
Glenburn High School

GETTING OUT OF BED IN THE MORNING!

Getting out of bed in the morning,
I can't help yawning,
Getting up for school, isn't at all cool,
Doing all the writing, and all the teachers biting,
Isn't much of a fab day, until I come home to stay.

Getting out of bed in the morning,
It can't be much more boring,
Didn't even close my eyes, I kept hearing little cries,
Strolling down the stairs,
Clutching my favourite teddy bears,
I pressed my finger on the switch,
And the brightness of the light made me, screw up my eyes.
That woke me up!

Dayna Turner (11)
Glenburn High School

HIGH SCHOOL

H itch a ride with your mum to school
I   gnore the teachers about the rules
G one in a flash after quarter-past three
H igh school is not the place to be.

S ummer holidays are nowhere near
C halk is on the board with an awful snigger
H orrible teachers just nag and nag
O n and on until their faces sag
O n holiday I would rather be
L iving the good life and having ice-cream.

Leann Irwing (12)
Glenburn High School

MRS CAT

Mrs Cat is very fat
And really likes to sleep
Everyday she lazes around
Just like a baby sheep.
Mrs Cat's fur is fluffy, and very white
You can see her coat in a dark night.
I told you that she's very fat
For some reason she is light
Yesterday, she nearly died in a fight
(with the neighbours dog)
It gave me such a fright!

Mrs Cat's a lovely cat
And I love her so
I am dreading the day that she'll have to go!

Katie Hodson (12)
Glenburn High School

THE TORNADO

The tornado spinning, picking up
everything in its reach
Spinning, spinning
Dangerous
As can
be
Slower, slower it is getting.
Finally it stops.

Kirsty Dunn (11)
Glenburn High School

WORLD STAGE

The world is a stage,
On which we do act,
It ends in a rage,
As a matter of fact,
There are seven acts, or seven of age,
Written into our acting contracts.

The first of these ages,
Is being an infant,
This is the most primitive of the life stages,
Puking and crying, like a sad, sad delinquent,
Rolling around like monkeys in cages.

The second of these acts,
Is being a school boy,
Making new friends, learning new facts,
Hearing loads of new words like Oi!
Running around, having some nasty impacts,
On the way you see life, as being a boy.

The third of these acts, nearly half way,
Is being a lover in the high school boulevard,
Thinking about your girl, until the end of the day,
And posing to friends, or trying to act hard,
Wondering what next to do or say,
Waiting for your Valentine, so you can give her your card.

The fourth of these acts, we're getting quite wise now,
Is joining the army at the age of eighteen,
Telling the weather from the sight of a cloud,
And using guns to kill, with the permission of the Queen,
You now have the training, but ignorance is how,
You'll notice that it's just about time to leave.

The fifth of all this, is life in general,
Getting a job, and earning money,
The middle years, where family is central,
Corporate ladders which are quite funny,
Bowler hat club member, in London's Mall.

The penultimate act,
Is being retired,
Your bedtimes get earlier, with a dead silent tact,
As your body gets tired,
Will you drop that old contract?
At such a late stage, the body is hired,
To the illness of being not mentally intact.

The last act, as the family gathers,
Mourners in the crowd,
As the foam in your mouth lathers,
You're dead, and now, you are allowed,
To enter the green room, not that it matters,
Because, my friend, *you're dead.*

Mark Newby (14)
Glenburn High School

LIVERPOOL

L   oads of talent, loads of skill
I   n the area they give us a thrill
V   ery fast and very strong, nothing could go wrong
E   verton could not score a goal
R   igobert's record is on a roll
P   remier league standards are high
O   bviously Owen is recognised
O   ver and over again (stop for three seconds)
L   iverpool, eleven good men.

James Waugh (13)
Glenburn High School

THIS POEM HAS GOT ME STUCK

This poem has got me stuck,
Look at it, just look,
My writing is a mess,
But it is my best.

This poem has got me stuck,
Look at it, just look,
The words don't seem to fit,
I think of it bit by bit.

This poem has got me stuck,
Look at it, just look,
I can't get it to rhyme
And I'm running out of time.

Rachael Lawrence (10)
Glenburn High School

I WOULD BE GOOD IF I COULD

I would be good if I could try
Not to throw the teacher out
Although it's fun to mess about.

I would be good if I could try
Not to play around,
Putting a fart cushion on the headmaster's chair
How was I to know that he'd be there?

I would be good if I could try
Not to graffiti on my book
I am an artist if the teacher looked
At my version of Miss Pickfall's new look.

Robert Donohue (12)
Glenburn High School

THE LEOPARD

As the leopard moved silently across the jungle ground,
Knowing one sound could end his life
For behind him is man, and in his grasp is a weapon
Guilty of the deaths of many creatures.

His muscles tense, his eyes, like emeralds planted in golden silk
Wooosh, a bullet soars through the air piercing the sky.

His heart leaps, racing like a cheetah
He lowers his head and creeps more cautiously than ever,
His velvet paws pad tranquilly across the floor of the wilderness.

His eyes wide, as he spies upon the man, who lifts his victim and
A limp face rolls out of the man's clasp;
And his eyes widen still, his heart skips a beat; and he staggers from
his hiding place, daggers pierce through his heart and visions only
from hell flash across his eyes; for his closest friend,
His long lost relation, his mother; rests in eternal sleep!

Cairen A M Wealand (11)
Glenburn High School

LIVERPOOL'S LAST GAME

L   iverpool's last game is coming
I   t's going to be a toughie
V   s Manchester United everyone's ready for footy
E   veryone's ready for the match to start
R   oaring from the crowd as the players part
P   atrick Berger's on a run he's going to put one in
O   h no Scholes is by his side and he's punched him in the chin
O   h no Berger's stuck on the floor
L   iverpool have taken the free kick and Owen has scored.

Keith Nutbrown (12)
Glenburn High School

LET THE CHILDREN RULE

In the heat of the battle thousands died
Thousands cried.
Many were left without a home
Many were left all alone.

Which battle was this? I hear you say
Pick any battle on any day.
The lament is the same but
To some it's just a game.

A game of power, a game of might
Women and children suffer
The men go off to fight
For what some just reason?
Some just cause?

Can you justify the thousands dead
Thousands maimed or left alone
'It was just' that's what you said
'We'll build you a new home.'

Will you build me a new dad?
Make Mum happy instead of sad?
Repair the scars on all the hearts?
Heal the minds, repair the parts?

Will the peace last this time?
Or just until the next time?
Thou shalt not kill
Will our generation have the will?

The will to live in peace with each other
Call all men my beloved brother?
Or will we fight another war?
A war to end all wars?
A just war?

Let the children rule
They are far too sensible
To fight and ruin the planet
What is a line on a map?
A reason to fight?
Don't make us laugh
Let the children rule!

Michael Crowder (11)
Glenburn High School

CHOCOLATE

Chocolate is nice like sugar and spice
Chocolate is sweet, unlike my father's feet,
Chocolate is gorgeous, and I wouldn't tell a lie,
So go on eat some, give it a try.

Rebecca Pate (12)
Glenburn High School

THE BIG MATCH

F antastic fun, oh no it's
O ffside looks like they are going to score
O h dear I think I'm going to shed a
T ear my team is getting beat, oh wait here's
B arry on the way, hasn't missed a shot all season, it's
A goal? He
L obs the keeper
L eaps a defender, taps it in *'It's in, it's in, we win!'*

Jamie Murphy (11)
Glenburn High School

THE RACE

Waiting at the start gate
Tension is growing
Waiting for the light
Tension is growing
Will I be fast
Will I fall off
Five of us
Eager for pole position
The light is on
Straight off the start ramp
Sliding round the corner
Pedalling like mad
Jump coming up
Pancake, can, can, 360 degrees
Riding in the wind
Fighting for pole position
Sliding round the corner
Jump coming up
720 degrees, double can, can
Finish coming up
Sliding round the corner
Flying over the whoops
Fighting for pole position
I won, I won, I won.

Philip Hughes (13)
Glenburn High School

HUNTING OF THE FOX

I hear the tortured sounding
As long shallow barks and padding hooves enter my weary
boundary.

Setting my paws upon a lonesome path,
I glide amongst the passive trees,
Their slender branches strike my tender body,
Telling me I have no more future.

I'm pursued along my forthcoming path,
Jaws of gilt set behind me.
And many deaths from their despised claws.

My amber eyes open wide as I search for a slink passage that
shall never be known.
Reluctantly I turn and face looking pitifully into my enemies deep
mystical eyes, he turns willingly, and with his finger steers it
towards me.

Cautiously I take my final steps as once more to my ears the
tortured sounding I hear. Then I shut them my eyes tightly closed,
then dagger-like claws are set into my russet fur piercing into my flesh.
Angry jaws I hear as vicious teeth are set within my body,
Whilst diamond-like claws are set into my flesh
Taking one final breath I scramble sorrowfully upon my feet
And witheringly I lay my head on ground on which my parents
ended their path.

From my amber eye I see many hounds racing throughout the distance.
And there I lay, wondering if I shall end with an eternal sleep.

Amy Toole (11)
Glenburn High School

DOLPHINS

Dolphins get caught in the tuna nets
Dolphins get put in zoos as pets
Dolphins need to be in the sea
Dolphins need to be with the family
Dolphins jump up and do flips
Dolphins of course cannot do splits
Dolphins save people in the sea
Dolphins go to bed like you and me.

Samantha Daly (13)
Glenburn High School

NIGHTMARE

It's night-time and it's time for bed
When I go upstairs
I'll lose my head.

I'm all alone in the dark
I don't know what to do
There are monsters out for a lark.

I have shivers in every bone
I look high and low
I wish I were not all alone.

Tomorrow I will surely be dead
It's no use you see
There is a monster under my bed.

Carmel Gerrard (12)
Great Arley School

RUGBY

The game has started
The teams are ready
The Red Bulls
All of them steady.

The game is beginning
All in a clean shirt
But after just ten minutes
They're all covered in dirt!

Rugby is a man's game
All the men look tough
But better sports you cannot find
They never play too rough.

My favourite team by far
Is The Red Bulls in USA
I watch them on TV
And I'll see them for real one day.

Duane Bridge (13)
Great Arley School

RAINBOWS

Rainbows are colourful
Rainbows are nice and pretty too
The colours stretch over my house
Green, yellow, pink and blue.

And one day I know I will
Find the pot of gold
And then I'm off and you'll see
A sign saying house '*sold.*'

Karl Burrows (13)
Great Arley School

NEW HOPE, NEW FUTURE

N ew hope, new future -
E verywhere in the
W orld - as the different midnights swept westward

H appiness, and the
O pportunity of
P eace for
E veryone

N ew hope, new future, new
E nergy, new
W orld

F ull of joy and wonder - *the whole world*
U nited
T omorrow . . . all of
U s . . .
R eborn . . . into
E verlasting *love*
           . . . everlasting *hope*
              . . . everlasting *peace*

Samantha Dean, Martin Roberts,
Sarah Heginbotham & James Morley (15)
Great Arley School

SPRING

S un shining
P eople smiling
R unning children
I n the light
N ew life, new start
G ood feelings in our heart.

Mark Fort, Steven Dagger & Anthony Collier (14)
Great Arley School

WINTER

W ind blowing
I   ce cold
N o warmth
T ea and toast
E vening in
R oaring fire.

Colin Addison, Nicola Rawcliffe
*   & Kevin Simpson (14)*
Great Arley School

MY GRANDPA JOE

My grandpa Joe's so very old,
So very old that he's gone bald.
All he eats is mush that's out of date,
And finds it hard to communicate.
He never moves from the sofa,
He just sits there like a loafer.
He's wrinkled and as pale as a ghoul,
And sometimes babbles like a fool.
He wears the same clothes every day,
But I suppose that in a way,
My grandpa Joe's pretty nifty,
He always give me £4.50!
When he sees me he smiles with glee,
He always has looked out for me.
He may move slow and he can't jump high,
But grandpa Joe's one *hell* of a guy!

Luke Hesketh (12)
Highfield High School

MANCHESTER CITY

Manchester City, Manchester City, they're the very best
Manchester City, Manchester City, they're miles above the rest,
If you ever see them play, you're certain to have a good day.
When the players appear out of the tunnel, the atmosphere is
electric and fun,
When Weaver saves that terrific shot,
People sing and cheer alot.
It's the last five minutes my heads in a spin.
You don't know whether you'll lose or win.
When Kennedy runs down the wing,
My heart misses a beat,
Whilst I'm sitting on the edge of my seat.
When they score that vital goal you hear a very loud roar,
The opposite team is on the break,
You suddenly stand up and begin to shake,
Fearlessly Tiatto dives in,
He leaves the striker with a knock on the shin.
When you walk out of Maine Road with that one nil win,
You're as happy as ever with a cheeky little grin.
With world class players they're sure to win,
If they don't they'll try again.

Marc O'Donnell (12)
Highfield High School

FOOTBALL

My favourite sport is football
I play it all the time
I pretend I'm David Beckham
When I'm running down the line

I'd really like his wages
I like his style of life
But there is something I don't want
It's Posh Spice for a wife

If I play for England
I will go very far
Own a nice house
Or a very good car.

David Hassard (13)
Highfield High School

A SNAIL!

A slithery, slimy snail,
Slowly sliding, leaving a trail.
Across the garden there it goes,
Under the bush and behind the rose.
Over the wall and onto the tree,
Munch, munch, munch, eating its tea.
Through the soil, it meets a worm,
But away it goes, squirm, squirm, squirm.
Oh dear, it then began to rain,
The poor little snail was washed down the drain.
But out came the sun, and he was surely fine,
So up the pipe he then did climb.
Sliding across the dewy grass,
He saw a huge bird slowly pass.
The snail slithered out of sight,
And tucked up in his shell, nice and tight.
He headed to the apple tree to meet his friends,
Leaving slime along the twists and bends.
When he arrived he began to eat,
Talk with his friends and dance to the beat.
It was dark then, so alone he had to roam,
On that long journey, back to his home.
At last he could snuggle up in his house,
To read a book and chat with the mouse.

Stephanie Clarke (12)
Highfield High School

HALLOWE'EN

31st of October, 'Trick or Treat!'
It's the time of year when kids roam the street.

Asking for candy, maybe money too . . .
At this time of year it is the thing to do!

They knock at the door, then they say . . .
'Give us a treat or we won't go away!'

One after another coming once in a while
Dressed as witches and devils they've really got style!

When they go home, they wait to be fed
Then as it gets darker they all go to bed.

At this time the real witches come out
Along with the ghouls they cackle and shout.

Even some devils rise up from Hell . . .
To terrorise children and adults as well!

Some zombies rise up from being dead
They scare all the children asleep in their beds.

At six when the sun rises the ghouls go away
To rot as a corpse till next Hallowe'en day!

At 7am the kids come awake
To find it was all just a dream
Only to find to their utter surprise . . .
Today is the real Hallowe'en!

Nicola Braddock (12)
Highfield High School

I CURSE THE DAY . . .

I curse the day he came to stay at my house *(my house.)*
Every single thing he touched, was either broken or crushed!
What did I do? I screamed!
(Da, da da, da daaa.)
I curse the day he came to stay at my house *(my house.)*
Outside when it was dark and damp, I looked at my shining lamp.
What did he do? He broke it!
(Da, da da, da daaa.)
I curse the day he came to stay at my house *(my house.)*
After we had just been fed, he looked at my brand new bed.
What did he do? He broke it!
(Da, da da, da daaa.)
I curse the day he came to stay at my house *(my house.)*
I showed him my action figure; he looked at it and gave a snigger.
What did he do? He broke it!
(Da, da da, da daaa.)
I curse the day he came to stay at my house *(my house.)*
We played on 'Tomb Raider 2' - he took it for a Frisbee and threw.
What did he do? He lost it!
(Da, da da, da daaa.)
I curse the day he came to stay at my house *(my house.)*
I let him on my mountain bike, he drove it straight into the dike.
What did he do? He sank it!
(Da, da da, da daaa.)
He cursed the day he let me stay at his house *(his house.)*
Every single thing I touched, was either broken or crushed.
What did he do? He screamed!
(Da, da da, da daaa.)

Sam Workman (12)
Highfield High School

DREAM WAR

Lights, sparks, blood, death,
What can stop this unholy mess?
From the dying man,
To the guns that sound like a rattling can,
Everything goes black,
Then a sudden blitz attack.

The rough sound of a dog fight,
Can we win? We just might.
Out of the air a German plane,
Next we see a massive flame.
Cheers for the English all around,
Then that sound was suddenly drowned.

More planes coming in,
Everything was just so dim.
Then there was a screech in the air,
So piercing you had to be there.
Then I woke with a scream,
Would you believe it was a dream?

Mark Rimmer (12)
Highfield High School

SKATEBOARDING

Spinning, turning all around,
Doing tricks and falling down.
Grind and slide on posts and poles,
Making sure to dodge the holes.

360 degrees shove it to tail grab,
And kick flip to Indy then nose grab
Me on my board whilst the audience talk
Moves invented by Tony Hawk.

I'll do these moves in Hawk's honour,
Smith grind, hand plant and Madonna.
Going round, doing well,
Skating with Kareem Campbell.

I can't believe I have just won,
Now I'm the Yoz Mag champion.
I've done well, I've kept on track,
And I guarantee I will be back.

Matthew Smith (12)
Highfield High School

MY STINKING LITTLE BROTHER

I have a little brother called Sam
Who thinks he can do what he can
He thinks he's the best
But to me he's a pest
And not a nice chap to have around.

Early in the morning he charges into my room
He lands on my bed with a boom, boom, boom
I roll over to one side and shout 'Leave me alone!'
Then all of a sudden my mum shouts 'Hannah, the phone!'

I get chucked out of bed
With a thumping head
Leaving my brother behind
I answer the phone to my mate Jermone
And told him I'll meet him at nine
I go back to bed with a thumping head
Because of that *brother of mine!*

Hannah Lakhlifi (11)
Highfield High School

ALONE IN THE CITY AT NIGHT

Alone in the city at night
It really must be a fright
Nobody there, it must be a scare
Alone in the city at night

Alone in the city at night
It really must be a fright
All on your own, too scared to roam
Alone in the city at night

Alone in the city at night
It really must be a fright
With no clothes to wear
No home . . . who cares?
Alone in the city at night

Alone in the city at night
It really must be a fright
Life's full of hard knocks
When your home is a box
Nobody cares
But everyone stares
Alone in the city at night.

Stephanie Coole (12)
Highfield High School

DOLPHINS

Sleek and serene
Grey and graceful
Dolphins

Peaceful and playful
Friendly and fun
Dolphins

Clever and cheeky
Beautiful and bashful
Dolphins

Talkative and touchable
Happy and huggable
Dolphins.

Leanne Ralph (13)
Highfield High School

NORMAL MORNING

My mother shouts, 'Get out of bed!'
But I would rather hide my head.
She shouts again,
I do not stir.
She's back again
And counts to ten.

I have my breakfast,
A large bowl of Shredded Wheat.
It fills me up,
Right from my feet.
It fills me up,
Oh, what a treat!

It's time for school,
I get in the car,
Everyone I see goes 'Ha, ha, ha!'
It's stripy yellow and green,
Has 3 wheels and is my mum's dream.

But for me it's a nightmare.

Shaun Thompson (11)
Highfield High School

THE SIMPSONS

The Simpsons are a funny crowd,
They laugh and scream and shout out loud.
Bart is a very naughty lad,
He makes Homer really mad.
Lisa has got spiky hair,
But Homer's head is quite bare!
Homer works for Mr Burns,
He does silly things and never learns.
Baby Maggie likes spaghetti, it's yummy,
She sits all day and sucks her dummy.
Marge tries to keep the family together,
But most of the time she's at the end of her tether.
Moe serves out all the beer,
He is very pleased if you gather here.
I watch them on the telly twice a week,
It's the only time I sit quiet and meek.
I laugh at Homer and his belly,
I've got to go they are on the telly!

Gary Nicholls (13)
Highfield High School

HALLOWE'EN

Witches, skeletons, ghosts and goblins,
they scare me out my wits,
it's all to do with Hallowe'en
and playing naughty tricks.

We all dress up
and on the darkest night,
we knock on doors
and give people a fright.

Pumpkin heads, sweets and money,
my friends and I think it's rather funny,
broomsticks, cauldrons, teeth and bats,
I really don't like the evil black cats.

For you see it is about trick or treat,
smell my feet,
or give me something good to eat!

Happy Hallowe'en!

Tracey Olsen (12)
Highfield High School

TIGERS!

Tiger!
Tiger!
What a beautiful sight!
Yellow and black, some pure white.
The forests some live in get smaller each day,
But it's only a tiger.
        Who cares anyway?
The tiger hunts whatever it can,
Mostly animal, but sometimes man!
The tigers are nearly all gone,
Through progress, for fashion, for money you know!
But it's only a tiger.
        Who cares anyway?
You see them in safaris,
And sometimes in zoos!
But when they're all gone,
It's us who will lose,
But it's only a tiger.
        Who cares anyway?

Suzi Jones (12)
Highfield High School

MY BEST FRIEND, CARLY!

I have a special best friend,
I hope our friendship will never end!

Her name is Carly P,
And she's really nice to me!

We take turns to sleep at each other's houses,
And she always wears cool trousers!

Every other Saturday, we go up town together,
Depending on the unpredictable weather!

We always take lots of money,
Trying on clothes is sometimes funny!

We sometimes buy lots of clothes,
Jewellery, make-up, anything goes!

We walk around every single shop,
And like the saying, 'We shop 'til we drop!'

Towards the end of the day, we have something to eat,
But McDonalds, no one can beat!

At the end of the day, we catch the bus,
Everyone's so tired, they're making a fuss!

When we get home, we have a rest,
And show each other our clothes, that's the *best!*

By that time, the day is almost over,
And Carly's parents pick her up, in their Rover!

I then look forward to Friday again,
So Carly can sleep over, I hope it doesn't rain!

Carly and I are *best* friends,
And I hope it never ends!

Megan Speakman (12)
Highfield High School

GHOSTS AND GHOULS

Lying in bed at night
With eyes shut tight,
Ghosts and ghouls
Come out of wooden bark,
Creeping upstairs in the dark.
They stir, in the dead of the night
Hovering around to give you a fright.
In the day ghosts and ghouls
Don't come out to play
But lay in rest,
Planning for the night's affray.
Darkness falls and out they come!
Screaming, banging having fun.

All different shapes and sizes floating above ground
Some of them big and some of them round,
Fat ones bouncing around the room
The biggest making the floor boom.
The walls are shaking,
The ceiling's breaking,
Daylight is coming
The ghosts start running,
But I was never really afraid
Of that night of evil they made!

Matthew Postlethwaite (13)
Highfield High School

AMBITION

Sometimes I wonder what I could be,
A scientist, a vet or presenter on TV?
Perhaps an assistant or a pop superstar?
No, that's pushing it way too far.

What about a chef or an air hostess?
Could I handle all of that stress?
How about a reporter or even a nun?
But surely that wouldn't be much fun.

Could I be a model and go to Milan,
London, New York or maybe Japan?
That doesn't sound right to me,
So what ambition is my cup of tea?

Thinking of this is way too hard,
Perhaps I could own a coffee bar?
Should I be a great inventor,
That doesn't sound any better.

No, wait a minute now I see,
The ambition that best suits me!
Because I am a super prancer,
I would like to be a dancer!

Vicky Caine (14)
Highfield High School

THE SHARKS

Sharks swim in the deep blue sea,
They can swim for miles because they are free.
Looking and searching for their next bite,
Makes all the little fishes disappear from sight.
Starving and hungry the sharks carry on,
Only to realise the fish are long gone.

Next on their line, humans will do,
Bigger, stronger and harder to chew.
But it will be worth it to have a full tum,
Then they can relax and head for the sun.
Off to new places they will go,
Wherever they choose, no one will know.

Mark Livesey (12)
Highfield High School

ONE DAY

One day I want to travel the world
From China to Alaska
India to Thailand
And Egypt to Nebraska.

I want to sail the Seven Seas
And see the wonders of this Earth
I want to see everything
Between Africa, Asia and Perth.

I want to swim with dolphins
Along Miami Bay
And I wouldn't mind scuba-diving
Around the Caribbean Way.

Although I like the Tropics
And places I can tan
I wouldn't say no to Greenland
And meeting an Eskimo man.

All these things that I want to do
Go to Barbados and Tenerife too
Maybe one day my dream will come true
One day, maybe one day.

Lindsay Milner (12)
Highfield High School

SHOPPING!

I got on the bus to go to town
And what did it do? It chucked it down!
I got off the bus and took off my coat
And there in a window was a note.
If you're down in the dumps and feeling pale,
Then come and see our massive sale.
I knew that was the thing for me,
So I went to look what I could see.
I saw a pair of leather trews,
With a matching pair of shoes.
But 'cos I'd eaten all those pies,
Of course they didn't have my size.
I saw a top that was red and white
And yet again it was too tight.
In the end I bought a bra,
That's the only thing that'd stretch so far.
I looked at the door after I'd paid
And there were some kids from fourth grade.
I slowly headed towards the door,
With my head looking to the floor.
I took a deep breath as I walked out,
Ready and waiting for them to shout.
Luckily for me they did not see,
That the person who'd passed was actually me.
As around the corner came the bus,
I thought to myself 'What was the fuss?'
As I sat down, away the bus went,
My worries returned, my bus fare was spent.

Rebecca Hems (12)
Highfield High School

THE SOLDIER

Blood rushing, head spinning,
Pulse rising, heart racing.
They're catching up,
I've nowhere to hide,
What's that? It's a crate,
I can duck behind it.

Check my guns,
No bullets left,
Only a knife,
What use is that?
Check in the crate,
Nothing in there.

I can hear them now,
Breathing deeply.
They're looking for me,
About 10 of them.
Maybe more, lots more,
They're all looking for me.

They're next to me,
I'll take my chance.
Here I go,
Jump out slash, slash, slash,
Only one left,
Lunge with the knife.

All right, I got the high score,
Press enter to proceed to level 3.

Jonathan Lomax (12)
Highfield High School

MY POEM ON SCHOOL

Boys and girls go to school,
Don't forget children rule,
Boys mess about,
Girls work hard,
Lots of lessons, phew that's hard!
Moving around the school,
Very hard and you get cool,
If you're ill tell a teacher,
If you're hungry go to the canteen,
Don't eat loads if you've got PE,
But don't forget to be polite,
Or you'll get into a big, huge fight,
But if you're good and stay in school,
You'll be smart and really cool.

Leann Martin (11)
Highfield High School

GOLF

Golf is a sport played by many,
Although it can be played by any.

Out in the open, with no disruption,
Except for the birds and the rustle of trees,
Now and again there's a shout of 'Fore'
Be quick off your mark as you duck to the floor.

Over the bunker onto the green,
Keep the shots coming, nice and clean,
It's nearly all over, the 18th's in sight,
Two more shots, to *putt* it all right.

Lee Collinson (12)
Highfield High School

SCHOOLDAYS

Don't wanna go to school today,
I wanna stay at home and do things my way.
No more school, no more books,
I'd rather stay at home and take care of my looks.
Stay at home and do my hair,
Look my best with lots of flair.
Nails perfect, make-up too,
When I'm at home I find lots to do.
Magazines, CDs and videos to play,
To keep me busy all day.
Go to the cinema and to town,
Spent all my money, time to frown.
I might as well go to school,
As working hard is one of the rules.
Must go and try my best
And next weekend I'll have a rest.

Natalie Whitehead (12)
Highfield High School

HOPE

My little sister has a gorgeous grin
And a little button chin
Her face is perfect in every way
And that I can honestly say
She makes all of us happy
She's as pretty as can be
She is called Hope
She's so cute and divine
Oooh! I love that sister of mine.

Jade Robinson (13)
Highfield High School

WEATHER

I hate weather
It drives me to the end of my tether
It changes every day
But it waters the garden without pay.

I hate the rain
It is such a pain
It makes me very wet
So I run as fast as a jet.

The wind can whip into a gale
And blow around a hay bale
It never does as it's told
That's why it makes me feel so cold.

I'm scared of lightning
It is very, very frightening
It brightens up the sky
And even scares the bravest fly.

I hate thunder
Oh what a blunder!
It wakes me up in the middle of the night
And gives me such a terrible fright.

I don't like the sun
Because it melts my chocolate bun
It takes away all the water
But helps to dry a lot of mortar.

I hate the weather
It drives me to the end of my tether
It changes every day
But waters the garden without pay.

Jennifer Milburn (12)
Highfield High School

UNKAFUNKA

At the bottom of the deep, deep ocean,
There was a great commotion,
As to who was the king of the sea,
'Oh, who can it be?'
But one day out of the blue,
A fierce creature swam through.

With fins of steel
And the voice of a grinding wheel,
The great Unkafunka had returned.

As it passed through the coral
And growled like a bear,
The great Unkafunka sat on the shale.
It looked around and gathered up some eel,
Straightened them up and started singing with its voice
of a grinding wheel
And drummed on the rocks with the eels' tails.

With fins of steel
And the voice of a grinding wheel,
The great Unkafunka had returned.

He danced through the hours until there was no more sun
And then he carried on some more banging on his drum.
But now he had shown his true colours,
All the little fishes took their place
And danced through the hours of the night and day,
And all the little fishes make it their dream,
To become the funkiest fishes they had ever seen.

With fins of steel
And the voice of a grinding wheel,
The great Unkafunka had found his home.

Chris Pendlebury (13)
Highfield High School

BLACK MAGIC!

His eyes are like the greenness of the fresh new buds in the spring,
They twinkle like the stars in the midnight sky,
His fur blends in with the pitch darkness of night,
His swiftness is like the speeding arrow,
His nose is pink that shows he is there,
His face has a simple complexion of warmth feeling,
His mouth is kept shut, only opened for his meals,
His tail is long and silky, it curls at the end with a twist,
When he sleeps he is in a ball in front of the warm fire,
As he sleeps he is softly breathing very peacefully,
For some attention he will stand on his hind legs,
He always shows affection to his owners with a small purring sound,
For fun he will try to catch the wasps,
The only thing that I know is that he is my *Black Magic!*

Zoe Hill (12)
Highfield High School

THE WORK OF THE LIONESS

Prowling, the silent assassin stalks,
Focusing on its weak prey.
Unaware of the great danger ahead,
Until it's too late.
The lioness goes in for the kill,
She's gaining on her prey!
Then all is still, a successful hunt.
A roar of triumph.
The lions tear off great chunks of flesh,
Mouth dripping with blood all over,
Fighting for their right to eat and share.
The hunt is over.

Mai-Yee Chan (12)
Highfield High School

CRAZES AND FADS

Crazes and fads are quite funny,
They cause every child to go out and spend money.
Even if it's something they don't like,
Like a hundred pound bag instead of a bike.
They buy things because their friends have them,
They could save up their money and buy a real gem.
In a few weeks what they bought they will hate,
Don't worry, a new craze will come at a later date.
Until then start saving your money,
And buy what you want and not what your friends find funny.
If your friends start to laugh,
Tell them you're buying what you want and not being daft.

Matthew Barnes (13)
Highfield High School

AIR RAID

The moment you step outside,
Bombs come screaming down,
Your heart beat quickens,
Your pulse races,
I'm running nothing gets nearer,
Finally I reach the shelter,
The bombs are getting closer,
Killing people by the minute,
The sound of falling bricks,
Is ringing in my ears,
The whining an whistling,
Due to the bombs,
It's all because of Hitler,
Why do we have to suffer?

Sarah Jones (13)
Highfield High School

THE WORLD OF MANY DIFFERENT FACES

Of all the colours,
of all the races,
of all the people of the world,
of all the love,
of all the hate,
of all the wars that you shall learn,
let something good come of the wars,
from different worlds that turn to hatred
instead of love,
please let something good come of
the worlds with many different faces
and many different races.

Let, when the time comes,
when people put down their guns,
let the peace be at the lover's hand,
to guide and not let the soldiers stand,
with determination or hand in hand
and never let them stand in their old places,
in a world of many different faces
and many different races.

Rachael Thompson (12)
Highfield High School

2 PLUS 2 IS 5

Why is maths so hard?
It turns my brain to lard
It makes no sense, I must be dense
Add, subtract, divide

It makes me want to hide
In deepest, darkest outer space
Add, subtract, divide

I wish I weren't alive
I'd rather be a ghostly me than
Add, subtract, divide

Right answer, wrong answer
Left answer, long answer
It's not amusing, just so confusing
Add, subtract, divide
Still, 2 plus 2 makes 5.

Megan Edwards (13)
Highfield High School

MY LITTLE SISTER

I have a little sister,
Her name is Bethany Jane
And I'm sorry to have to say this
But she sometimes is a pain
She messes with my make-up
And tries on all my shoes
And when I tell her off for this
She runs to mum and boos.

She dances to my music
Dresses up and has a pose
But wouldn't you believe it
She does it in my clothes!

Although she does annoy me
She's nicer than my brother
And when she's not annoying me
I suppose, I really love her.

Jenny Conchie (13)
Highfield High School

FRENCH

French is so hard
It turns my brain to lard
All the le, la and les
And the une, un and des.

French is so hard
It turns my brain to lard
All the ta, ton and tes
And the ma, mon and mes.

French is so hard
It turns my brain to lard
All the Juin, Juillet and Septembre
And the Avril, Mai and Novembre.

French is so hard
It turns my brain to lard
All the dictionares, l'elagère and les stores
And the le tableau, l'ecran and le placard

French is so hard
It turns my brain to lard
Why is it so hard?
Why can't it be like English?

John Watkins (13)
Highfield High School

WILD CAT

As the night draws in,
And the stars are in the sky,
Out comes the wild cat,
Sleek and sly.

His eyes glow up green,
And his fur is jet black,
He looks awfully mean,
As he sneaks down the alley back.

Kaylie Brocklehurst (12)
Highfield High School

THE LIGHT

It is warm
It is bright
It is a storm light

I can see it
I can be it
I can feel it in my toes

They think it's good
They think it's bad
They think it's full of joy
But sad

It was my friend
Good to give and to lend
That had to in the end
With a message of hope to send

Don't be hurt or alone
Don't be sad or be mad
Don't be a fool, be fair
Because the light will be there.

Jade Hamer (13)
Highfield High School

COMPUTERS

Computers at school
Computers at home
Computers everywhere
Are usually very cool, surf the Internet
Look under games, sometimes just a name
My favourite site
Is coffee break arcade
Which has games
Where you run through blockades
There's also a site MP3.COM
Which has music on
It makes you rave
It makes you groove
It really, really makes you move.

Andrew Flanagan (13)
Highfield High School

TIGERS

Tigers come in different sizes,
They all come in orange and black stripes.
They roar loudly
And prowl slowly,
Until they see an enemy,
To which they run
And pounce and eat them in one gulp.
They really are amazing.

Sarah Anderson (11)
Highfield High School

MY BROTHER

I have a brother and everyone thinks he is cute
But the brother I see is a little brute
He sits around all day watching TV
Lazy as ever, leaves everything up to me!
When he wants feeding he screams and shouts
'Give me some food otherwise I'll go into your room
and throw your stuff out'
'Oh yes!' I replied back
And with that he threw a lot of food at the cat!
'Look what you've done now,' I said catching a cereal box
'Hurry up child and get the mop!'
Carefully he mops the food up with care
Does he speak he doesn't dare
Hours later he's back at the TV screen
And I thought to myself, 'How mean!'
But of course I wouldn't swap him for no other
Cos after all he is my brother!

Emma Purvis (11)
Highfield High School

SCHOOL

I like school
It's great, it's cool!
All the people
Are such fun
Well maybe not everyone
I like school
It's great, it's cool!
Especially Highfield High School.

Allia Howard (13)
Highfield High School

WINTER

Stood at the far side of the school playing field,
The wind howling into my ears and through the trees as if a hurricane.
The sound of dissoluteness.
The only moving objects: a few pupils walking across shivering on
their way home,
And litter blowing around with the wind.
Too cold.

Walking down the path by my old school,
Dragging my feet through the leaves to hear the pleasant
crackling sounds.
The sound of winter's approach.
The only living things: a few dew-covered weeds poking out of
the ground,
A few people driving past in cars.
Sad, yet happily content.

Sat in the back room,
Staring out the window while my sister plays behind.
The sound of each raindrop hitting the cold glass like winter's
voice making itself heard,
The only sense of duty toward my sister calling me from behind.
Grateful, warm and content.

Turning round from my paper while writing this poem,
The only sounds the clock, rain and computer whirring away.
Quiet, relaxed, grateful, content, happy.

Scott A Silburn (13)
Highfield High School

A POEM ABOUT NETBALL

Running onto the netball court,
I feel excitement of some sort.
Standing in my 'centre' position,
Winning the game is my ambition.
The whistle goes, I make a pass,
The other team has no class.
Fifteen minutes in '4-0'
was the score,
Our team kept on shooting
more and more.
The final whistle blew
and every body knew,
That we were the best,
Better than all the rest.

Lauren Oldland (11)
Highfield High School

THE SADNESS OF WAR!

War is terrible and so sad,
War is horrible and so bad.
People in pain and crying,
Soldiers in the trenches dying.
Big bombs falling overhead,
People lying still and dead.
Blood all over the place,
A crooked moustache upon Hitler's face.
The sound of guns firing,
Silence people are admiring.
War is terrible and so sad,
War is horrible and so bad.

Thomas Higgins (12)
Highfield High School

SPACE

In the galaxy above there are nine stupendous, glittering planets,
Billions of twinkling stars that are miles and miles away,
Satellites from NASA peeping at the moons,
Burning meteorites whirling through the gigantic universe,
The tremendous *sun* gleaming all year round,
The planet *earth,* so minute compared to the galaxy,
The spiral, sparkling Milky Way so far away,
Comets flashing through the sky.

There are many things in space,
Although there are many more things to be found!

Sean Hamer (11)
Highfield High School

I'M A MONSTER

When I awoke this evening,
When all things were dead,
A bat flew onto my arm,
It vanished because I ate the little guy with bread.

When I awoke this evening,
When all things were dead,
A little boy came in and sat next to my own,
He vanished because I sucked his blood.

When I awoke this evening,
When all things were dead,
A mob came in my armament,
They all vanished because I ate them.

All that because I'm a *monster!*

Mark Wright (13)
Highfield High School

FAITH

When someone steps out,
You feel cold and alone.
When someone steps out,
You feel numb to the bone.
They aren't really gone for long,
They aren't really gone at all.
But you feel,
Like the barrier, the wall,
That it won't be broken,
You won't see them again.
You don't believe in heaven,
This is now, that was then.
The person you loved, admired and respected.
That person's gone forever,
You now feel neglected.
But friend, why feel this way?
Instead, very simply,
Just remember the days,
You shared together,
The laughter, the tears.
You will prosper without them,
Into different careers.
You will go along the road of life
And they will be there.
All along they are watching,
They did and will always care.

Nicola White (13)
Highfield High School

IN THE FUTURE THERE IS ONLY WAR

In the future there is only war
Aliens screaming and dribbling slime
Space wolves snarling and biting
Eldar jumping and flying around
These are the enemies of the Imperium

A loud thundering boom, a crash, a flash of light
Then the sound of a door opening
And a tall shadow appears
He steps out onto the war-torn floor
And a booming footstep follows
More and more shadows pop out one by one

They are the space marines, the fighters of justice
Who will not stop until everything that opposes him is dead
Terribly out-numbered they still fight

A boom, boom, boom in the distance
The sound of gun fire echoes around them
They charge into battle, armour shining, guns blazing
Who only care about killing the enemy

Blood of a thousand creatures rests on a single marine's hands
And he only wants even more
But it's too late for him
After the dust clears, the only things visible are
The thousands of bodies on the floor
He's the only one left
The blood of his comrades is up to his ankles
But the blood of his enemy is up to his knees

He has won the battle
Yet he feels so alone, empty and sad
When he should feel righteous

Stephen Rhodes (13)
Highfield High School

I'M NOT IN THE MOOD!

I'm not in the mood for going to school,
I'm not in the mood for obeying rules.
I'm not in the mood for listening to teachers,
I'm not in the mood, the feeble old creatures.

I just want to sit at home all day,
Not going to school, wasting my youth away.

I'm not in the mood for going shopping,
If you think I am you're mad and hopping.
I'm not in the mood for pushing a trolley,
It's wet outside, I'd need a brolly.

I just want to sit at home all day,
Not going shopping, wasting my weekends away.

I'm not in the mood for going to work,
Dressing up in a suit, looking like a jerk.
I'm not in the mood for going to that meeting,
It feels like I'm getting a right old beating.

I just want to stay at home today,
Not going to work, wasting my life away.

I'm not in the mood for retiring,
I want to go and do some filing.
I'm not in the mood for collecting my pension,
When you get old, partying's out of the question.

David Atherton (13)
Highfield High School

AIR RAIDS

We were all sitting
down for tea,
we were having
biscuits and cheese.

Then we heard the
mighty sound,
Father came running
down.

'To the Anderson
shelter,
or you will feel
that bomb belting!'

Inside the shelter
it was cold and damp,
I just think about
the concentration camps.

The all-clear siren
had gone off,
but when we went out
all we did was cough.

There was dust
all around,
and lots of rubbish
on the ground.

People's houses had all
but gone,
all because of one
single bomb!

Christopher Skinner (13)
Highfield High School

FROSTY MORNING

Cock-a-doodle-doo,
A cool, cold winter sun rise,
Car wind screen full of settled frost,
Frost on each house window melting into freezing water,
Curtains closed in every house, in every window,
Grass hard, sharp and white from frost,
Birds singing their own soothing songs,
Trees bare and gardens full of leaves,
Puddles full of ice floating around with the sun rise reflecting off it,
Streets silent, it is as if the world has been deserted,
Drip, drip, drip, the leftovers of the rain,
Woof, woof, dogs bark out loud,
Cats just waking up with a big yawn,
Beep, beep, suddenly the curtains opened,
People stare out of the window at the end of the frosty morning.

James Benson (12)
Highfield High School

WHAT IS A POEM?

A poem can be fun some days
A poem can be dull some days
A poem can be good in a way
Or even bad in one day
A poem could be fun
Or even about the sun
A poem could be long
A poem could be short
But over all a poem is a poem
And that's all I've got to say.

Christopher Lindley (12)
Highfield High School

THE SWIMMING RACE

I get up on the blocks,
The starter says 'Take your marks, *go!*'
I'm off, into the water I go, kicking my legs as hard as I can.
I'm swimming really fast,
I take a breath to the side I'm winning.
Into the turn I go, up onto the surface I go,
I'm swimming harder than ever.
My arms feel like they're going to snap in half,
But I'm getting closer to the wall.
I hit the wall I've won the race.
Hooray!

Ben Penswick (11)
Highfield High School

THE SKY

The sky is all sorts of colours,
Black, blue and grey,
It shines through the day,
And glistens through the night.
If you think about it,
It's quite funny really,
How it's either shining or dull.
And it really gets me when
There's a quick flash of lightning,
And then a shower of rain.
Then when morning comes,
The sun comes out again.

James Atwell (11)
Highfield High School

MY CAT

The cat is called Suzi
She's a little brat
The cat is not fat
She's a little brat
The cat is black
She's a little brat
The cat has a white chin
She's a little brat
The cat scratches the dog
She's a little brat
The cat bit me
She's a little brat
The cat plays with the ball
She's a little brat
The cat runs around the house
She's a little brat.

Jason Lee Wilkinson (12)
Highfield High School

THE SUN

First you add the sauce to stop the meat from burning,
Then it cooks you like a giant flaming oven.
It turns up the heat, looking over it's human pieces of meat,
Then the heat cools down when the meats nice and brown.
It turns off and the flames go down.

Oliver Byrne (13)
Highfield High School

THERE ARE FAIRIES AT THE BOTTOM OF MY GARDEN

There are fairies at the bottom of my garden,
I haven't seen them but I know they're there.

Every night when I go to bed I look out of my window,
I see lots of bright lights in the bushes at the bottom of my garden.

The other children laugh at me at school
And say that I'm a liar,
The teachers don't believe me and neither do my parents.

But I know that there are fairies at the bottom of my garden,
Do you?

Karly Louise Duckworth (12)
Highfield High School

THE ANIMAL

This animal is blue and smooth,
Its life is spent in the cool waters of the sea,
Its voice sounds like a little mouse squeaking,
This animal is the best swimmer on the sea's surface,
It is not friends with the shark, so he stays right away,
He eats little tiny fish that live deep down in the dark waters.

> Can you guess what it is?
> *A dolphin!*

Danielle Heckman (11)
Highfield High School

A SPOOKY TALE

I have a ghost who walks round my bed,
Moaning and groaning 'it does in my head'.
I've asked him quite nicely to please go away,
But each night at midnight he comes back to play.

He jingles and jangles and bangs on the door,
He jumps on my bed till I fall on the floor.
It's getting so night-times I'm starting to dread,
I would kill him if he wasn't already dead!

I thought a big dog would keep him at bay,
But he frightened poor doggy which then ran away.
Call the armed forces or call the police,
I'm so tired, I need to rest in peace.

My mind is scrambled, I tell my friend Kate,
I can't remember the day or the date.
When the spectre just seemed to walk into my life,
To cause me such pain, trouble and strife.

Then just last Tuesday a vision in white,
Walked into my room in the deep dead of night.
My mysterious spectre ran for his life,
These words faintly heard 'My lord, it's the wife!'

My tale has ended, I've no more to say,
I've had no more trouble since that fateful day.
My sleep is so peaceful it is quite a bore,
Can someone at least bang on the door?

James Hush (11)
Highfield High School

RACING CARS

Your average racing car,
can't travel very far,
on roads and motorways,
cos that's what the rule says.

Your average racing car,
can travel very far,
always on the attack,
round and round the track.

Your average racing car,
smashing into the bar,
blows into lots of bits,
then it's back to the pits.

Your average racing car,
roaring across the tar,
speeding towards the line,
to them, winning is divine.

Nick Parker (12)
Highfield High School

GRANDMA JUNE

Grandma June is a cheesy old prune,
Cos every night she's dancing with a broom.
She eats her apples with a spoon,
Then goes to bed with a balloon.
Every morning she's in bed till noon,
And when she wakes up, she badly needs a groom.
Everyone thinks she's a lovely racoon,
But I know that she is a big baboon.

Joe Ramsden (11)
Highfield High School

STARTING HIGH SCHOOL

I was nervous starting Highfield
It filled me with such dread
I would have done anything
To stay at home in bed.

My parents bought the uniform
They said high school is great
I went to bed real early
Scared that I'd be late.

I really like my high school
The teachers are just fine
My form tutor is the best
I'm glad that she is mine.

Lee Turpin (11)
Highfield High School

FISHING

I went fishing on a bright sunny day,
The water was gleaming and the air smelt of hay.
The sun was shining as bright as can be,
I set up my fishing tackle under a tree.

I cast out my fishing line close to the edge,
And while I was waiting I ate a sandwich.
I felt quite a tug on the end of my line,
My rod was bent but my line was fine.

My rod was still bending, what a fearsome fish,
If it's a trout it will go on a dish.
If not a trout then maybe a plaice,
Whatever it is I'll have a smile on my face.

Michael Bramhall (12)
Highfield High School

LIVERPOOL FC

Football is my favourite sport,
And Liverpool's the team I support.
Fowler, Gerrard, Heskey and Owen,
They always try to keep on goin'.

Barmby came from Everton,
From blues to reds,
Good on ya' son.

Liverpool is my best team,
And to play for them is my dream.
I like to watch them on TV,
Cos Liverpool's the team for me.

I play for a Sunday league team,
South Shore is their name.
We got to the cup final last year,
And lost, it was a shame.

To play for Liverpool,
That's my dream.
But for now,
I'll just play for my team.

Luke Paterson (11)
Highfield High School

NIGHT OF THE DEAD

The sky was dark
And the air was still
The silvery mist
Cast a deadly chill

Out of the graves
The spirits rose
And glided downhill
In shimmering rows

For down this hill
The victims lay
The villagers slept
Till the break of day

As the ghostly mob
Performed their dance
The helpless towns folk
Were put in a trance

Silently their leader
Raised his wicked head
And proclaimed that this
Is the night of the dead.

Amy Duxbury (11)
Highfield High School

MY TEACHERS . . .

My teachers are snotty, drooling, tyrant-like creatures,
Not at all like normal teachers.
They come up close and laugh in people's faces,
Shouldn't they be in a home for nut-cases?
Then the bell rings for my break,
And suddenly I'm wide awake.
Then I'm back in my classroom,
And I have an impending sense of doom
Because I remember I have DT,
And now I've forgotten my kit for PE.
All pm I've looked forward to that last bell,
So I can go home and escape from this living hell.
An evening of freedom and a good night's sleep.
But then my alarm goes off, with a loud beep.
And I know, I have to face the teachers once more,
Oh! What a bore!

Thomas Tribick (12)
Highfield High School

OLYMPICS

Olympic fever has gripped the nation,
We all tune in on the TV Station.
With medals galore for athletes to win,
There's so many sports my head's in a spin.
Fencing, boxing and swimming too,
If you come first it's the gold for you.
With teams competing and spirits running high,
Even if you lose, you've still had a try.
So all you losers, go back and practise,
In four years time you may have cracked it.

Liam Atkinson (13)
Highfield High School

HARMONY

I feel safe
Huddled here
Watching the centuries go by
A cool, calm sea
Waves lapping gently
Bringing more room for
Generations upon generations
To pass over the water
To pass away and finally live in
Harmony.

I feel safe
Knowing that a wall
Twice the size of me
Is supporting me
Helping me to see a
Generation looking towards
Harmony.

There is no end to peace
Souls walk from cool to freezing
Sea turns to ocean
Ocean turns to eternity
I want to pass away
Leave the wall
And live in harmony.

Kate Madigan (15)
Kingswood College At Scarisbrick Hall

SPACE MAD

I feel like a comet,
Or a shooting star,
Entering a race,
Driving a flying car.

Engines roaring,
Blasting off at the speed of light,
The car is soaring,
In the middle of the night.

Passing places ever so far,
Mercury, Saturn and Jupiter.

Stars in formation,
The way to our destination.

We won the race!
Everyone was slower than my pace.
I will close my eyes
And pick my prize.

Hannah Richmond (11)
Kingswood College At Scarisbrick Hall

MY HOME TOWN

Southport, a town on the NW coast
full of character, people and the odd ghost
created for gentry who liked to swim
in this millennium were they clever or just dim.

Lord Street, a street with all posh shops
where they sell everything including pork chops.
There is a place for the kids called the fair
and a place where women can do their hair.

In parks in summer you can hear a brass band
or lie in the sun on the soft sand.
Pubs and bars you cannot leave in haste
hotels and restaurants with catering for every taste.

That sums up Southport
in just a few words.

Matthew Ball (11)
Kingswood College At Scarisbrick Hall

LIFE

No scientist can give a logical yet scientific
Explanation for the thing we all live.
And indeed I am no scientist, nor a poet
However read on and I shall explain
A teenage point of view, of life.

Life is what we all live, a thing we take for
Granted.
One minute you're here, yet tomorrow
You might not be.
Life can be cruel I know that for a fact,
Life can be generous and then it is not.

We should all live our lives to the maximum
For one day they shall end
And you will think in your head
'All the things I did, yet all the things I could
Have done,'
But it's too late. Your life is over. Gone.
So live, live your lives
Because time is ticking by
If you're not careful
Time will take it from you.

Francesca Barker (13)
Kingswood College At Scarisbrick Hall

HATRED

Hatred is all around us in every possible way
In our feelings, actions and often in what we say
Many say dislike, hate is such a strong word
Though it hurts people have never cared
To know you're hated is not worth to know
Because the hurt inside of you will never go
And as you would indeed find
It's like a stone weighing down your mind
Clouding each and every thought in your head
From when you get up to when you go to bed
Every minute and second that goes by
You can't think of anything but the question why?
Why, what did you do to make them feel that way?
To hate you forever every day
The feeling of hatred will always be with you
No matter what you try and do.

Dominique Fuentes (13)
Kingswood College At Scarisbrick Hall

MY HOMEWORK!

English, maths and science too,
So much homework for me to do,
I rush home every day,
To get it done and then go play.

English is to read a book,
So I'll just have a quick look,
Great, that's done, now what's next,
To get on with the text.

Maths is to do addition,
It really is a mission,
Get the calculator from the case,
The question is 'How long was the race'?

Science is to use your brain,
Or else, it will be the cane,
Physics, chemistry and biology,
Is all too much for me.

Thomas Taylor-Hampson (11)
Kingswood College At Scarisbrick Hall

GAMES WITHOUT FRONTIERS

Isn't life a lot like chess?
The strong and the weak,
All under stress.

Valiant knights fighting in battle.
While the rooks and the pawns,
Are herded like cattle.

And there a white queen,
Will sit on her throne.
Whilst beside her the king, will mumble and groan.

On and on, they battle in vain,
For the victory is one,
neither may gain.

But not so in life,
Chess is only in fun.
For down here on Earth, black and white are as one.

Nadine Andrews (13)
Kingswood College At Scarisbrick Hall

AUTUMN

Autumn is a quiet time
Where leaves turn green to red
And as I walk through the park,
The leaves fall around my head.

The sun shines briefly in the sky,
The wind begins to blow,
The clouds are rushing past,
The sun is getting low.

The wind blows through the drying leaves,
Which makes them swirl around,
I continue to walk,
The leaves fall without a sound.

Hannah Sinclair (12)
Kingswood College At Scarisbrick Hall

FREEDOM

Freedom is a wonderful thing,
Freedom a lot of happiness will bring,
Some people's freedom has been taken away
But I still have mine to this day.
People have fought for theirs in wars,
While others are forced to obey the laws,
Prisons are totally packed,
With people whose behaviour has sadly lapsed.
November the 11th is Remembrance Day,
To those who cared, our respect we pay,
To all those who died in both World Wars,
Freedom the reason . . . Freedom the cause.

Stephanie Tope (11)
Kingswood College At Scarisbrick Hall

HARVEST FESTIVAL

Shush, we're ready to start,
Did you hear that? Quiet Mark.
Sam it's your turn to go,
Hurry up, don't be so slow.
Ann - careful with those eggs,
Whoops, too late, they're all down your legs!
Amy will you please stop staring
It is *not* a dress that the vicar is wearing.
The grapes are for harvest, John
But now they are nearly gone.
But thank you all for your fruit and things,
Now sit back while the choir sings.

Hannah Towers (11)
Kingswood College At Scarisbrick Hall

ICE PALACE

The cold, crisp air,
Surrounds me,
As I walk silently,
through land,
forever lost,
no scenery,
covered by a crunchy blanket,
fish covered,
by a glass of ice,
glaciers like ice cubes,
moving slowly,
my palace,
my home,
of ice.

Charlotte Rimmer (14)
Kingswood College At Scarisbrick Hall

MY HOPES AND DREAMS

I dream of a mansion
Of my very own,
With 200 rooms
At my very own home.
Two Jacuzzis and a swimming pool too
And even my own designer loo!
My job as a pop star
For a million pounds a day,
A husband rich and handsome
To look after me in every way.
The world would be a peaceful place
With no more wars or fights,
With love, peace and harmony
And to want whatever's right.
Plenty of food for everyone
With sickness a thing of the past.
My hopes and desires are for these to come
True . . .
And for them to last and last and last.

Kate Johnson (11)
Kingswood College At Scarisbrick Hall

HAUNTED

House of night, house of dark
I heard a scream or was it my mind?
Under the floorboards something lurks
Tonight we will see.
End of reality, end of Earth.
Deadening silence, a thought unturned.

House of horrors
And where spirits dwell
Understanding this house is hard enough.
Tonight we will tell
End of life
Dead or alive.

Rachel Handley (11)
Kingswood College At Scarisbrick Hall

FOOD

Food is delicious and tasty to eat,
Some may be sour and some may be sweet.
Apples, bananas, pears and grapes,
These are a lot healthier than curry or crepes.

Chicken, turkey, beef or lamb,
People prefer these to sausage or ham!
Crisps are salty, as are chips,
There are millions of varieties of salad dips.

Cakes and biscuits are lovely and sweet,
We usually have these as a tasty treat.
Eggs, yoghurt, butter and milk,
Are always tasty and as smooth as silk.

Pizza, pasta and lots of garlic bread,
These are the foods that you'd like to be fed.
Some food is healthy, but some food is not,
Food is served cold and food is served hot.

Food is on a shelf in tins and cans,
To help prepare it we use pots and pans.
Food can be found anywhere: near or far,
Such as in a cereal box or a small jam jar!

Stephanie Ross (11)
Kingswood College At Scarisbrick Hall

HUMPTY DUMPTY!

Humpty Dumpty sat on the wall
Was he pushed or did he fall?
The whole event came as a big surprise
Oh how the king's men did tell such lies.

Oh dear it really is a shame
Humpty wonders who is to blame!
Sitting in hospital stitches and all
Now Humpty can't go to the eggtastic ball.

They called in the doctor, they called in the vicar
From Humpty's eyes there wasn't a flicker.
Poor old Humpty didn't look well
But was this a crime only Humpty can tell?

They sit by his bedside all eager to hear
About this vile creature who has brought so much fear.
When all of a sudden Humpty started to mumble
Perhaps at last the criminal they will rumble.

Who did it, who pushed you they began to cry?
Come on Humpty don't tell a lie.
Humpty sat up no longer near death
As the rest of the town all held its breath.

The person who pushed me works for the Queen
It's someone that you will all have seen.
He's naughty and sly and nicks jam tarts.
Yes, you've guessed, it's that Knave of Hearts.

Charlotte Read (11)
Kingswood College At Scarisbrick Hall

WAR

War, what is it?
No one really knows.

The world so full of hate and pain,
The battlefields driving me insane.
People killed with a single shot,
Then the bodies are left to rot!

Anger in the families mourning,
People dead without warning.
The noise of tanks, bombs and guns
Then the machine guns' piercing hums!

Keep low down, a bullet skims your head
Bang! The major is suddenly dead.
What do you do? Panic, run or even cry.
Or do you just lay down and die?

But why can they not resolve this without fighting?
Can't they put it into writing?
Just talk about it, what is the point of war,
Can't they just abide by the law?

Down the trenches men must stay,
Until the war ends on a glorious day.
Many are laid to rest,
The people must protest!

Let the innocent stay alive,
Then just let peace arrive!
War, what is it?
No one really knows.

Sarah Singleton (13)
Kingswood College At Scarisbrick Hall

THE WILD MUSTANG

Swishing tail,
Wavy mane,
Thundering hooves,
Glistening eyes,
Galloping into the orange, red sky.

A silhouette standing in the breeze,
A riderless horse watching, waiting, contemplating,
What should he do next?

Cantering swiftly over the ground,
Don't stop, don't turn around.
Dangers lurking round every corner,
Nothing scares him as he ventures further.

In the distance his goal awaits,
Not much further he estimates.

Charlotte McRae (11)
Kingswood College At Scarisbrick Hall

ODE TO PETROL

O petrol
O petrol where have you gone?
We miss you
We need you
We all think as one.
Without you we have nowhere to go
Without you we have no friends to visit.
No food, no bread, no wheat, no heat.
I wonder what we are going to eat?

Was it really so bad?
Fewer cars on the road
One week with clean air
People talking about 'you'
I'm glad I was there.

Elina Poulimenou (11)
Kingswood College At Scarisbrick Hall

MY EARLIEST MEMORIES

I remember my first smell of roast chicken.
It smelt crisp and fresh
It was spitting
And crackling violently in the oven.

I remember my first taste of Calpol.
It tasted sweet,
Fruity and sugary.

I remember when I was younger the sound
Of the police sirens.
They buzzed
Howled and hissed
As they flashed by.

I remember when I was younger the first
Time I had stroked a horse.
It felt smooth,
Silky, soft
And velvety.
Their mane felt rough
And dry.

Rachael Majakas (13)
Kingswood College At Scarisbrick Hall

WAR OF THE WORLDS

The UFO landed without a sound
And people gathered all around
A cylinder from out of the sky
Lay quiet and still close by.

In time the cylinder opened up
And people waited to have a look
They should have kept away with fear
For the Martians invading Earth are here.

They came out fighting with machines they'd made
People ran everywhere for they were afraid
They tried to conquer us with all their worth
Unaware of the fatal bacteria on Earth.

Christopher Taylor (11)
Rossall School

GET ME IT

I want a bike,
Get me it.
I want a doll,
Get me it.
I want a cat,
Get me it.
I want a dog,
Get me it.

Mum, I want a bike, a doll, a cat, a dog
Mum, can I have them?
Please! Please!
Mum can I have them?
No!

Claire Glassey (11)
Rossall School

SICK

My tummy is turning over like a washing machine,
I look in the car mirror and look a tad green.

I shouldn't have eaten all those cream cakes,
sticky buns and chocolate too.
Because now I feel I'm going to spew.

Sorry Mummy, didn't mean it and I'd better clean it.
I no longer feel sick.

Aimée Rutherford (11)
Rossall School

THE RACE

On the starting line
Oh what a thrill
Heart's beating fast
Makes me feel ill.

Tension is mounting
Whistle will blow
Push off back foot
Raring to go.

Running fast
Wind blows my hair
Must keep pushing
Finishing line's there.

Over in minutes
Work all done
Excitement is over
I'm number *One*!

Mark Howard (12)
Rossall School

SOMETHING IS SOMETHING

Something is something
but never the same thing.
Something is something
and always the same thing.

Something is
the worst thing in the world
but
it can also be the best.
Something is
before the match
when the opponent stares at you,
you stare back
and win the match.
Something is
what you feel
when you have just lied,
when you could have told the truth
or
at least you could have tried.

Something
is the best thing in the world
but
it can also be the worst.

Something is something
but never the same thing.
Something is something
and always the same thing.

Theodore Pengelley (12)
Rossall School

I REMEMBER

I remember summer
With the warm, golden beach
The calm sea by my side . . .
But then
I remember
The strong, wet, tropical storm
That blew you away.

I remember autumn
With the orange, red and brown
The brambles and apples . . .
But then
I remember
The cold winds that chill
Everything to the bone.

I remember winter
Playing in the white snow
The thought of Christmas . . .
But then
I remember
The wind and rain and sleet
That makes everyone bored.

I remember spring
The fluffy lambs playing
Flowers beginning to grow
The cold chill going away
The thought of Easter eggs
There's nothing wrong with spring
Nothing at all . . .

Ileana Lund (12)
Rossall School

MIND OF A POET

What should I write?
I don't know
Should it rhyme?
I don't know
Should it be funny?
Should it be sad?
All the answers
I don't know.

Where should I start?
I don't know
How should it end?
I don't know
Should it be short?
Should it be long?
All the answers
I don't know.

Should there be passion?
I don't know
Should there be hatred?
I don't know
Should it have heroes?
Should it have villains?
All the answers
I just don't know.

Lewis Allen Dingle (12)
Rossall School

ALLBIENALLE

All the millions of people in all the
        countries everywhere,
            Are treated as an equal, yet we have the
            chance to step out with our own flare.

Some people like to sing and dance, and
        others prefer to paint in France.
Many I know make money with plays, a
        few even take each talent, by phase.

Some people have crooked noses to smell
        themselves out of fear,
Others have big, bright eyes to show
        when they're full of cheer.

We're different, in how we think and act
        we're different in how we look and feel
        we're different in every aspect of life
        and that is what keeps this world real.

Earth would be so boring,
Earth would be so plain,
If all the people were the same,
that is why we are unique and
find differences every day.
Getting on with one another and
challenging life in a variety of ways.

Jennifer McCormack (13)
Rossall School

THE FINAL TRY

It was the last day of the season.
We had to win the game.
We were leading the league tables.
We had to make a name.

The other team said 'We'll beat you'
But we knew they never could
We played like maddened tigers in a darkened wood.

We ran and battled fearlessly
And scored the winning try.
We knew that we could do it
'We are the champions,'
All the team did cry.

We collected our cup and medals
And paraded around the ground.
Everyone in the stadium
Stood up and shouted
'Lads, you've done us proud!'

Daniel Hignett (12)
Rossall School

BLACKPOOL ZOO

Blackpool Zoo is the place for you,
Mums and children all come too,
Animals there for all to see,
Especially the monkey climbing the tree.
Elephants there, big and tall,
Eating leaves, big and small,
Peacock with its wonderful wings,
Children can see them when they swing on the swings.

Nicola Wrathall
St Aidan's Technology College, Poulton Le Fylde

WORLD WAR III

All the leaders of the world gathered in one place,
One from every country, each religion, every race.
They all sat down together and it was very plain to see,
That something must be done about the recent tragedy.

Spain invaded Holland, which upset Germany,
But this greatly pleased Greece and Hungary.
Brazil attacked Argentina, much to their dismay,
A few days later the whole world was in disarray.

Russia blamed Spain; they had started it after all,
Some said it was the fault of tiny Senegal.
England believed that Bolivia was to blame,
And though opposed to England, Turkey thought the same.

A solution was needed that would please everyone,
But no one seemed to want to even try to reason.
A truce had to be made and they had to think of a plan,
And something was proposed, by the leader of Afghanistan.

'There's lots of room in space but one problem, no air!'
So inventors were called in to find out how to breathe up there.
After one week a solution was found,
Everyone was excited for it was space that they were bound!

The inventors then produced one more fantastic creation,
A spaceship that could carry the people of every single nation.
The people of Bulgaria were the first to board the shuttle.
And once they were seated, in the others scuttled.

They never made it to space, they had barely taken off,
When the people of France said everyone else was soft.
They all started fighting and soon they were all dead,
Why didn't they just try to sort their differences out instead?

Simon Gill (12)
St Aidan's Technology College, Poulton Le Fylde

AUTUMN

Autumn is a plate of exotic food,
It is full of different flavours,
I get into my outdoor clothes,
The hat on my head is a warm furry cat,
The gloves two of his paws,
My coat is big and cosy like a big, black bear,
The crispy, golden leaves are batter under my feet,
The sky is a thick, black blanket,
As I walk along the damp, lamp-lit road,
The smells of bonfire night fill the air,
Murky puddles everywhere like miniature lakes,
The bonfire is a comet shooting into the sky,
The fireworks are like bursting rainbows,
They dance through the sky,
Teasing the passers-by,
Guy Fawkes propped up in the fire,
Sparklers and luminous rings, twinkling like stars,
Autumn is a plate of exotic food,
It's full of different flavours.

Morwenna Howell (11)
St Aidan's Technology College, Poulton Le Fylde

OUTSIDER?

What is an outsider classed as?
Is it a black?
Or is it a person in a chair?
I don't know, but I'm sure they care.

People don't care about them,
They shout at them,
Just because they are different,
They just don't care if they cut them out.

They are bullied, day in and day out,
They feel left out.
They feel as if they are not there,
Sometimes, as if they don't belong.

People should feel for them,
They do no wrong.
They just want to fit in the world
And so they should, because they belong.

Stephanie Parkinson (12)
St Aidan's Technology College, Poulton Le Fylde

THE AUTUMN FOREST

I walk through the autumn forest,
I hear twigs crack
And the wind whistles.
Leaves flutter down like birds
I see a hedgehog in a pile of orange leaves,
The rotting leaves smell musky.
I touch the conkers fallen on the ground,
Smooth and glistening in the light.
The sun sets
The sky turns a reddy-orange with a rosy hue.
When it gets dark,
The fireworks start
And turn the autumn leaves blue.
I taste the ashes on the breeze,
Coming from the bonfire party.
When the night is over,
Soggy, fireworks are left
Ashes cover the ground,
Everywhere smells of smoke.

Phillipa Beames (12)
St Aidan's Technology College, Poulton Le Fylde

ROBOT WARS!

The mayhem of metal
Why not try the Sumo Basho?
So let the trials begin!

Chaos 2, that flipping ramp,
Mortis with an axe.
Hypnodisc, that shiny thing,
Sergeant Bash will fry you to a frizzle!

Razor will slice any chassis,
Pussycat always lands on its feet.
King B3 and the ramming spikes of fate,
Matilda's tail could cut your little finger off!

Dead Metal will pinch you,
Sir Killalot will take you to the pit.
Shunt will push you with a snow plough,
Whilst Refbot roams about the arena!

Who will come victorious,
In the Robot Wars heat?
Start with six, end with one,
Until next time; Goodbye from Robot Wars.

James Hesketh (12)
St Aidan's Technology College, Poulton Le Fylde

THE OUTSIDER

You look, you stare especially at my hair
I can't help having ginger hair.
So why do you look, stare and point?
It's only hair, the only difference is the colour.

What did I ever do or say to you?
To make you dislike me, nothing!
So please stop looking and laughing at my hair.

Glen Anderson (12)
St Aidan's Technology College, Poulton Le Fylde

SMUGGLERS POEM

I was in my bed fast asleep,
I heard a noise outside,
I was so tired I could hardly move,
I wish sleep would come soon.

I tossed, I turned,
I pulled my pillow over my ears,
But I still could hear the noise,
I wish sleep would come soon.

Should I get up and have a look,
No it's far too cold.
The floor will be cold on my feet,
I wish sleep would come soon.

I still wasn't asleep and midnight came,
But I think I had a dose,
Did I get up to have a look, no it had been a dream,
I wish sleep would come soon.

Sleep won't come I must get up,
The floorboards feel so cold,
I wipe the frost from the window,
I see my dad carrying barrels, oh no it can't be!

Lee Jenkinson (12)
St Aidan's Technology College, Poulton Le Fylde

THE TRAMP

The sound of shuffling shoes,
across the concrete floor.
The smell of stale booze,
as he passes by our door.

Is he lonely
where does he go?

We see him every day
'How can he live like that?'
You hear the women say,
as he counts his money in his hat.

Did he ever dream his life would be so rough,
Did he ever dream his life would be so tough?

Emily Hargreaves (12)
St Aidan's Technology College, Poulton Le Fylde

THE DIFFERENT KINDS OF PEOPLE

Tall people, small people
Big kids, little kids.
Laughing, joking and snide remarks
Hurts people's feelings sitting in the park.
Running with their heads hung down
People shout names and then kids frown.
Missing out on games and always last in line,
How do I cope with all that slime?

Abbey Mealor (12)
St Aidan's Technology College, Poulton Le Fylde

AFRICAN BEGGAR

Black, white what a race.
Big nose, small eyes, what a face.
Disabled or a squashed-up face.
Why have we got such a funny taste?

Learning disabilities, a drama queen.
A mathematician, a tear from a black woman's face.
A dog with one leg, a cat without a tail
An old woman, a young boy with a funny taste.
Why have we got such a funny taste?

A boy with only two fingers, a girl with only one toe.
An old woman, a young boy with such a funny taste.
A stamp collector, a six foot tall boy
Why have we got such a funny taste?

Daniel McMillan (12)
St Aidan's Technology College, Poulton Le Fylde

FLOODS

Winter is coming and we've started to fear what is near.
The television shows it's awash in the south,
thank goodness we are all up here.
The rain came gushing, rushing and broke the guttering.
The roads disappeared as we feared, fields were flooded
and hills became muddied.
Rivers and streams merged as we observed.
Is this a sign of things to come?
We thought it was glum with no sun.

Brett Helme
St Aidan's Technology College, Poulton Le Fylde

ALONE - REMEMBER WHO YOU ARE!

He sits there,
Waiting,
Waiting to be loved.

His face is covered with curly whiskers,
The dirt building up
Looking like death!

He told me once,
Remember who you are.
I didn't get it.
I wish I had had the courage to go back.
He's gone.
I still don't get it.

Why did he say that?
That's the question I've asked myself,
Remember who you are.

I'm older now
Kids of my own, I say to them
Remember who you are!

They don't get it,
I don't,
He didn't.

Rachel Warnock (12)
St Aidan's Technology College, Poulton Le Fylde

SMUGGLERS

On the edge of the Cornish coastline
Nobody would say that the day was fine,
The sea roared over the rocks
But has not seen the birds flock.

In the small town of Tintagel
The smugglers were out in the town.
Waiting for people to open the curtains
Then hide round the back and leave some brandy
Mix it with lemonade and have some shandy.

Then one day they find a shop
They nip in to get some pop
They steal it from the server's counter
And run away in great, excited laughter.

The smugglers find a place to hide
So the police don't find them who aren't on their side
And they would tell King George himself,
Who will take them to prison himself.

The smugglers were trying to dodge tax
And that is not too good, I thought,
They steal something from a shop
And I hope there is not brandy round our garden
So I certainly don't want smugglers in this town.

Richard Eite (13)
St Aidan's Technology College, Poulton Le Fylde

GINGER HAIR

I knew Holly was getting bullied
I heard her crying at night
I was getting very worried
They must have given her a fright.

It must have been her ginger hair
We've got Irish blood in us
She couldn't talk to her friend Claire
All the questions in my head buzz.

One day after school she came home
Her eyes were red as the sun
She tried to fight back on her own
Then she had a fight and Jordon won.

When Jordon saw me she ran away
She never comes to our house
I know she will come back one day
I still see her as a little mouse.

I knew Holly was getting bullied
She has me to help her now
I don't ever have to worry
Just think I've beaten Jordon '*Wow*'.

Danielle Whitehead (12)
St Aidan's Technology College, Poulton Le Fylde

HALE-BOPP

In the sky burning bright
You can only see it in the night
A firework called Hale-Bopp
Is a speeding icy rock.

Spinning round the world it goes
And where it stops nobody knows
One hundred and twenty three
Million miles away
I wish we could see it every day.

Jack Bramhall (11)
St Aidan's Technology College, Poulton Le Fylde

THE WEDDING DAY MEMORIES

Velvet, cotton, silk and lace,
Being a bridesmaid for a day is ace.
You can hear the bells ringing
And the echo of children's voices giggling.

Cake, pop, discos galore,
Going home is such a bore.
I loved the day when I
Felt like a princess.

I love to throw rice
And all things nice,
Watching it as it falls like snow
As the newly married couple go.

I listen to the speeches,
As I eat my cream and peaches
And look at the towering
Cake, covered in cream and icing.

As the day is done,
We see the setting sun,
I am dreaming of the time,
When that wedding day is mine.

Penny Bostock (11)
St Aidan's Technology College, Poulton Le Fylde

THE DRAGON AT SCHOOL

I can always remember the great, big scare,
At school once, when a dragon was there,
It must have come from its giant lair,
But it wandered around without much care.

Then there was a massive fright,
When the dragon breathed with all his might
And the school all set alight,
It really was a dreadful sight.

So if at your school, a dragon appears,
Don't think it will be there for years,
There is no need to shed any tears
And after all I have told you, please don't have any fears.

Rachel Graham-Dickinson
St Aidan's Technology College, Poulton Le Fylde

FRIENDS

Friends are our friends for a reason
To share out thoughts and secrets with
Friends are our friends for a reason
To look out for us always.

Friends are our friends for a reason
For them to sleep at mine and me to sleep at theirs
Friends are our friends for a reason
To help us with our work.

Friends are our friends for a reason
To whisper to in class
Friends are our friends for a reason
That reason is that they care!

Penny Gladwin
St Aidan's Technology College, Poulton Le Fylde

My Pets

This is a poem
About my pet family,
Two dogs, a cat
And a pony.

One of my dogs is called Joker,
He likes to joke around,
The other one is called Katie,
She is Joker's matey.

Then I am going
To move on
To tell you about
My cat.

So my cat is called Kay,
She messes around
And plays all day,
That's what my cat is like.

The last pet I am
Going to tell you about
Is my pony
And what he does.

My pony,
He is not a tall, bony,
He is a Shetland,
Westlife is his favourite
Pop band.

Kate Ganderton (11)
St Aidan's Technology College, Poulton Le Fylde

HALLOWE'EN

On a dark and stormy night,
The ghosts come out and give me a fright.

I walked along and I saw a witch,
She came past me and I fell in a ditch.

I ran home as scared as I was,
I knew I had a price to pay that was.

I shouted McBeth on stage,
I thought nothing of it and thought of my age.

Knock, knock on the door,
I ran along and slipped on the floor.

I opened the door, the face was hairy,
It was all moulded and scary.

'Who are you?' I said
'Don't worry I'm not dead.'

I'm sorry you are.

Vincent Scott (13)
St Aidan's Technology College, Poulton Le Fylde

THE WAY TO GO

What if how, what if why
What if I could touch the sky?
Would it be the way to go
Would it be the way I know?

If I should go I mean,
I would leave behind my past
I should go and never return
That's if I knew it could last.

Help me God to find my way
Or just to show me the light
I really need to know,
I need to know today,
If you can't then I will have
to show them I can fight.

Hannah Pears
St Aidan's Technology College, Poulton Le Fylde

FEELINGS

Happiness
Happiness is bright sunshine yellow
And tastes like a freshly cooked breakfast.
It smells like a fresh bouquet of flowers
And looks like a clear Caribbean beach.
Happiness sounds like birds humming in the early morning
And feels as though you are floating on a cloud.

Anger
Anger is burning, hot red
And tastes like spicy chicken.
It smells like burning fuel
And looks like a row of burning houses.
It sounds like a fierce tiger
And feels as though you are going to explode.

Sadness
Sadness is deep, dark blue
And tastes like a rotting apple.
It smells like mouldy cheese
And looks like screaming faces.
Sadness sounds eerie and quiet
And feels as though you are all alone.

Karley Smith (12)
St Aidan's Technology College, Poulton Le Fylde

TEN POUND NOTE

A ten pound note as crisp as paper,
Its eyes seem to follow you
It has not much colour
Just a bit of orange, grey, white, black, brown, blue.

A ten pound note is worth a lot of money,
Yet only a piece of paper.
With some writing and pictures printed,
And with it a lot of things bought,
Yet only a piece of paper.

A ten pound note is just a piece of paper,
That to people it seems so hard to keep.
But if it is so valuable,
Then why is it so easy to rip!

Mark Frost
St Aidan's Technology College, Poulton Le Fylde

AUTUMN

The leaves have dropped off the trees,
Different colours,
The smell of poppy fumes,
Dew on the grass,
Leaves smell of soda,
Children picking conkers,
The sky is reddy-orange,
Leaves are crackling,
Hedgehogs hibernating.

Leigh Connolly (12)
St Aidan's Technology College, Poulton Le Fylde

TEDDY BEARS

They're cute and cuddly,
Soft and woolly.

> Everybody loves,
> Nobody hates.

Big and small,
Fat and thin.

> Everybody loves,
> Nobody hates.

Big paws, soft paws,
Small paws, hard paws.

> Everybody loves,
> Nobody hates.

They come in different colours,
Multicoloured to snowy white.

> Everybody loves,
> Nobody hates.

Bill, Lil, Phil,
Toffy, Rolly, Cutie.

> Everybody loves,
> Nobody hates.

And don't forget Rupert and
Paddington Bear.

> Everybody loves,
> Nobody hates!

Becky Davenport (11)
St Aidan's Technology College, Poulton Le Fylde

BUBBLES

Leaping over the sea
Like a diving bird,
Her bubbled skin
And spiky fin..
Bluey, grey.

Under the sea,
Speeding through
The deep, green weeds
Teaching her newborn calf
How to swim.

Jetting through the
Turquoise sea,
Riding along boats,
Racing the others.
Feeling free.

Jumping as high
As the sky,
Showing off her tricks.
Who are those people?
Pointing and taking pictures.

Kirsty Shaw
St Aidan's Technology College, Poulton Le Fylde

ASHLEY MY BROTHER

Ashley is my brother,
He's the loudest of us all,
He fancies loads of girls,
He has a friend called Paul.

My brother Ashley,
Reminds me of a brick wall,
He thinks he is good looking
But he looks like a sick mole.

Natalie Russell (11)
St Aidan's Technology College, Poulton Le Fylde

A NEW BEGINNING

Of the many animals of the world,
the tiger is down to *one!*
Hiding in a bare, steel cage,
his life is one big con.

His shiny coat no longer shines,
his stripes no longer sharp.
Heavy eyes, claws grown in,
a cry, his mourning heart.

But then one day a flood of hope,
pumped through his every vein.
An almighty leap, one mighty roar!
He is free and free of pain.

Off to the jungle he escapes,
he hunts, to find a friend.
A beautiful beast just like him
the tiger has evolved again.

Two roars echo throughout the land,
soon joined by hundreds more.
My dream of the tiger's great return
its beauty, its deadly claw.

Sara Whalley (12)
St Aidan's Technology College, Poulton Le Fylde

BONFIRE NIGHT

Toffee apples nice and sweet,
These are such a tasty treat,
Watch the fireworks in the sky,
They light up the corner of my eye,
Banging, frapping as they go
These fireworks are never too slow.
The fire fraps and crackles too,
It burns the wood and rubbish through.
Treacle toffee ready for me,
I don't want to spoil my tea
Catherine wheels spinning round,
Making a lovely whirring sound.
The fire finishing, burning through,
Guy Fawkes is dead and burning too
The smell of smoke lingers through,
Treacle toffee has gone too.
Say goodbye for another year
Guy Fawkes ashes to earth, listen you'll hear!

Fireworks!

Karen Swarbrick (12)
St Aidan's Technology College, Poulton Le Fylde

ROLLER-COASTER

I feel the tension and the strain,
Our cart is going up again,
We are waiting for the big drop,
I think my heart is going to stop.

Up and up and up some more,
I don't think I can see the floor,
All around it's very misty,
Or I myself am very dizzy.

Here it comes; it's nearly time,
I really feel like I could die,
I'll not look down, I'll not think twice,
I think I will just close my eyes.

Down and down and down we fall,
Just like a great, big, round ball,
Oh, I wish this ride wasn't so tall . . .
Actually that wasn't so bad at all.

Helen Metcalfe (12)
St Aidan's Technology College, Poulton Le Fylde

AUTUMN

The bare trees,
Sway silently in the breeze.
The dry crispy leaves
Dance on the dewy grass
Before they are raked up
Into peaks of flaming colours.
The fireworks are like brightly coloured
Butterflies,
Exploding in the charcoal sky.
The swallows twitter excitedly like school children
About their long journey home.
The squirrels happily scurry around,
Collecting acorns which have fallen from the
Ancient trees.
Harvest gifts decorate the village churches,
Accompanied by choruses of 'We plough the
Field and scatter . . .'
Farmers relax knowing their crops have been
Safety stored.

Rebecca Morgan (11)
St Aidan's Technology College, Poulton Le Fylde

VOICES IN THE NIGHT

Lying in bed awake,
Looking at the wall,
Thinking of my father,
Gathering at the mall.

I hear funny voices,
Out on the road.
Want to go and look,
But I can't or I'll be took.

I dare to go and look,
Only peep around the cloth.
Can't believe my eyes,
My father's right outside.

I move from my window,
Feel a draft of wind.
Father's in the house,
As quiet as a mouse.

I quickly jump in bed,
Pretend to rest my head.
Try to think what Father did,
With the other men.

I think about the story,
My father told me last.
About the Gentlemen,
Suddenly it comes to me.

Father's a Gentleman,
Clear and plain as day.
That's what he wants to do,
When I'm old enough to sew.

Emma Gardner (12)
St Aidan's Technology College, Poulton Le Fylde

SMUGGLERS

I wake up,
I hear voices,
I walk to the window,
I hear voices,
I see horses.

I see father,
Carrying a barrel,
I see uncle,
Carrying a barrel,
Leading a horse.

I see mother,
At the gate,
Watching the men,
From the gate,
Counting barrels.

I see the priest,
Pushing a barrow.
I see the butcher
Pushing a barrow,
Carrying a light.

I hear a whistle,
I turn to look,
See a pony.
I turn to look at
Silhouettes on the hill.

A mad scramble
Running men, galloping horses,
On the hill, the silhouettes move in,
It's all gone,
I go back to bed.

Emma Canning (13)
St Aidan's Technology College, Poulton Le Fylde

DANCING DREAM

Tomorrow is Saturday,
My favourite day,
I pack my shoes
And am soon away,
It's dancing class,
I'm rushing to,
I have a Jazz lesson to do,
I run on in, I'm there at last,
The class is large, the music fast,
It's such good fun with all my friends,
But all too soon the lesson ends.
I change my shoes and have a rest,
Next is Ballet I love that best.
Blocks in my shoes, up on my toes
Just for a while, the teacher knows
I can't stand long on points just yet,
But never mind one day, you bet,
I'll be a famous dancer grand,
My name will be known throughout the land.
I've lots and lots of work to do,
I'll practice till my toes are blue,
So just watch out, in future years,
After lots of falls and many tears,
A promise to myself to fill,
My name in lights,
Top of the Bill!

Sarah Gillette (12)
St Aidan's Technology College, Poulton Le Fylde

THE SMUGGLERS

Suddenly, there were noises.
The squeak of a wheel and whispering voices.
I woke from my sleep
And decided to peep
Out of the window
And onto the street.

When I looked out the window
And saw them below,
There were people moving ever so slow,
The butcher, the baker, the candlestick maker
People and horses and so many barrels.
But oh so quiet,
Like they were frightened.

Then someone turned and looked up to my window,
To my horror I saw,
My father,
What should I do? Should I hide?
I rushed back to bed
And I closed my eyes.

My heart was pounding,
I should be asleep,
But my mind was full of the sights I had seen,
It could not of happened,
My father is good,
I decided that it must of been a bad dream.

Joseph Booth (12)
St Aidan's Technology College, Poulton Le Fylde

AUTUMN

Autumn days when the grass is jewelled,
With the colours of brown, red and orange,
Heavy conkers falling from trees so high,
And the smell I sense the most is of the autumn leaves.

Hedgehogs hibernating here and there
With the fumes of the flowers in the air,
The colourful autumn night sky
Along with the summer sun saying goodbye.

Ripening fruits for harvest time,
Now's the time for robin redbreast
After his long seasons rest,
It's time for the birds to say goodbye,
As they fly in the autumn morning sky.

Donna Hopkins (12)
St Aidan's Technology College, Poulton Le Fylde

MY GARDEN

When I look out of my window
In the garden nothing stirs
A cat wanders through the
Gates and very gently purrs.

At dusk the garden is still
In high winds the grass blows wild
The leaves on the trees rustle
In the summer it's quite mild.

I love my little garden when nothing ever moves
When over the garage there's hanging, red leaves
Growing down the side
The wooden hut buried under the dark, grey trees.

When I look out of my window
In the garden nothing stirs
People say whose is that?
That garden, that is hers.

Kelly Giles
St Aidan's Technology College, Poulton Le Fylde

WINTER AND SPRING

Winter comes but once a year,
Although she's cold she brings great cheer.
She blows on everything, coats them in frost,
Nearly Christmas things are starting to cost!

She blows on the rooftops and the ground,
Covering them in a white blanket all around.
She silently, softly moves away . . .
For spring he is approaching, sunny and gay!

Spring is happy, full of fun,
He makes everybody want to run.
The lambs, the chicks are born this time of year . . .
But summer is coming and she's full of cheer!

Ashleigh Monaghan
St Aidan's Technology College, Poulton Le Fylde

ICE-CREAM VAN

Ding-dong, Ding-dong,
Here comes the ice-cream van,
Ding-dong, Ding-dong,
He is such a kind man.

'Mum, Dad, can I have 50p?
I really want an ice-cream,
Can I please?
Thanks Mum, thanks Dad' - with a cheesy grin I beam.

Open the door,
Slam shut,
'Naughty boy' shouted Mum,
'Tut, tut, tut.'

Running down the street,
Like I was totally mad,
When I had that ice-cream,
Boy would I be glad!

Three people in the queue,
Lots of time to decide,
Would it be the 'Crackpot' with bits of crackling candy?
Or would it be the 'Fizzler' with sherbet inside?

It's my turn now,
I'm all for the Fizzler 'cos it is my fave',
But the 'Mixxy' looks good,
For the peanuts I crave.

Well I've decided it's the 'Mixxy'
It's the obvious choice,
So I order it up,
With a breathless voice.

David Robson (12)
St Aidan's Technology College, Poulton Le Fylde

SMUGGLERS

The noise awoke me
Coming from outside,
I did not know whether to peer out
Or to jump back and hide.

I drew back the curtains
And peered round the side,
Then it was that I saw him!
My father was outside.

There were carts and horses,
All of the village was there.
In with them was my father,
As busy as the village fayre.

My father stood in the middle,
Wearing his black cloak and hat.
People were creeping and whispering
No time to stop for a chat.

Large barrels seemed to be loaded
Onto a cart at the back.
Pulled by our black stallion
Driven by the stable boy Jack.

Eyes wide I watched it closely;
It went to the magistrate's door.
He patted my father whilst winking
They'd never seemed friendly before!
My heart and spirits were sinking,
What they were doing I wasn't sure.

Sophie Woods (12)
St Aidan's Technology College, Poulton Le Fylde

FLASH, CRACKLE AND SPARKS

Flash, crackle and sparks,
Children and sparklers light up the gloom.
Squeaking and squealing as they go,
Bang, sizzle and boom!

Flash, crackle and sparks,
Catherine wheels spinning round.
Flashes of light, light up the dark,
Fireworks - boom!

Flash, crackle, sparks alive!
Over, under, through and dive.
Flash, crackle, sparks alive!
Bang, sizzle and boom!

Craig Collins
St Aidan's Technology College, Poulton Le Fylde

THE SAME AS YOU

I really am no different, just
Because I was born blind.
If you'd take the time to talk to me
Then I know you'd find
I like the same things as you,
Music, clothes and boys.
Just because I can't see them
Doesn't mean I can't enjoy.
So please do not ignore me,
Include me in your game.
Don't leave me on the outside
Just because I'm not the same.

Kim Lawrenson (12)
St Aidan's Technology College, Poulton Le Fylde

THE WORM'S DECLARATION

I am the worm.
I live in darkness.
Never seeing light.
If you were to pluck me out of the soil,
I would wriggle and squirm,
But I would not see you.
I would not fight.
For I am the helpless worm,
Who lives in darkness.
Never seeing light.

Yes, I am the worm.
I live in darkness.
Never seeing light.
If a bird were to catch me in its beak,
I would expand and go limp,
But I would not see it.
I would not fight.
For I am the worthless worm,
Who lives in darkness.
Never seeing light.

But if you were to see me in my darkness,
I would surprise you.
For I can move without limbs.
I can navigate without eyes.
And I can live after murder.
For I am the helpless worm.
The most amazing of all creatures.

Kirsty Kelly (13)
St Aidan's Technology College, Poulton Le Fylde

DREAMS

Dreams last forever,
Yet where will they lead?

Life and reality turn to dust as you dream,
But when you wake the dream disappears.

Tears fall as you lose the dream you reached for,
As you had it snatched away.

Memories are all you have, all you can see.
To touch a memory is a dream in itself.
To mix a dream with reality,
To touch what you lost as you woke
And make a fresh start; lead a new life.

Dreams carry and will lead you to your destiny.
You dream your dream and it will be carried.

It is your perfect world, your dream.
Never let anyone take that away.
Take your dream, snatch it; for your dream is the
reality and if you grab your dreams,
Hold them with a tight fist.
They will always come true,
Your dream becomes your life.

Hannah Taylor
St Aidan's Technology College, Poulton Le Fylde

AUTUMN

Crunching, crinkling, crackling, leaves
Hear the sound under your feet,
Here comes autumn again.

Rusty, autumn gold, orange, leaves
See lots of different colours,
Here comes autumn again.

Cold, wet, windy weather
The weather's getting colder,
Here comes autumn again.

Bang, crash, boom go the fireworks,
Bonfire night is here
Here comes autumn again.

Marie Murphy (13)
St Aidan's Technology College, Poulton Le Fylde

SHOW TIME!

It comes along only once a year,
Five times in one week,
Parents, grandparents all come,
To see children tap their feet.

In ballet we wore
Pretty white socks,
Peachy coloured shoes
And multicoloured frocks.

For tap, I wore a purple leotard,
A black waistcoat with gold trimmings,
White tap shoes and then
The lights started dimming.

So lots of people
Came to see,
Lots of different dances
And in the interval, had a cup of tea.

One year to wait,
Till we perform again,
Who knows if I'll be in it,
Next year we'll know, but now I'll have to go.

Stephanie Hume (11)
St Aidan's Technology College, Poulton Le Fylde

THE SMUGGLERS OF PENZANCES WOOD

The moon shone brightly in the velvet sky,
I hear footsteps, I wonder why?
I drew back the curtains and there they stood,
The smugglers of Penzances Wood.

The clicking of the horses, the smiles on their face,
Five men in all, was it some game or race?
The leader was rich, dressed in red and black,
The man behind carrying some kind of sack.

People glared as they passed by,
Frowning anxiously with a hateful eye.
They crept round the corner as quietly as they could,
The smugglers of Penzances Wood.

I drew back the curtains, time for bed,
I closed my eyes and in my head,
I saw a familiar face,
It was that man in that game or that race.
Maybe I should just forget what was seen and was said,
But I couldn't.

Jenny Patten (12)
St Aidan's Technology College, Poulton Le Fylde

AUTUMN

Conkers are clonking
Acorns are plonking.
Leaves are crackling,
Cider is packing.

Halloween will scare,
Trees are bare.
Dew is on the grass,
Leaves flutter past.

Bonfire night,
Fireworks are bright.
Sky's rosy-hue,
Flowers are few.

Hedgehogs hide,
Birds fly.
Mist drops,
Noisiness stops.

Tracey Hogarth (12)
St Aidan's Technology College, Poulton Le Fylde

AUTUMN POEM

Autumn is cold
And it is cool
Because it is the time of
Year for bonfire night
And lots of other great
Events
The fireworks go off with a bang
Like a gun being shot
Around me
The fire crackles like
Leaves being walked on,
The colour of the fire
Changes from red to yellow
And back again.
At Hallowe'en your house is
Visited by children
Dressed as ghosts and witches
Wanting sweets for Hallowe'en.

James Smith (12)
St Aidan's Technology College, Poulton Le Fylde

HALLOWE'EN

As the pumpkin man creeps through the hedge,
The witch rides again.
With the hollow sounds of the trees,
The mummy's reborn,
The vampire attacks with fangs.
As the ghost shows his blushing white face,
The zombie moves around looking for someone to scare.

With the high cackle of the witch
And the mummy's low-pitched groan,
The zombie shrieks,
The vampire weeps,
And the ghost appears again.

As the rose flows,
A new soul is in Heaven.
As Satan cries,
The werewolf dies
And Hallowe'en is over again.

Andrew Hodgkinson (12)
St Aidan's Technology College, Poulton Le Fylde

MY DAD WENT TO WAR

I played with my dad,
I laughed with my dad,
I lived with my dad,
I shared with my dad.

I said goodbye to my dad,
I hugged my dad,
I kissed my dad,
I waved farewell to my dad.

I missed my dad,
I prayed for my dad,
I cried for my dad,
I hoped for my dad.

I waited for my dad,
I found my dad,
A cross, my dad,
A poppy, my dad,
I loved my dad.

Samantha Ratcliffe
St Aidan's Technology College, Poulton Le Fylde

SMUGGLERS

As I opened the curtains,
For the very first time.
I really wanted to see,
What Dad's been hiding all the time.
Never for me to see!

I saw my daddy passing barrels,
Along the big long line.
I did not know what he was doing,
But I thought it was fine.

Then I saw him going to the ship,
He came back struggling.
Carrying a crate of beer,
Then I realised, he was smuggling.

I'm really very worried,
It's a very dangerous thing.
What if he gets caught
And gets taken to the king.

Stephanie Ronson (12)
St Aidan's Technology College, Poulton Le Fylde

AUTUMN

Autumn is the time of year,
Full of fun, laughter and cheer.
Leaves are falling to the ground,
Lightly, softly without a sound.
Conkers are protected by their spiky shell
And children search the ground where they fell.
A layer of leaves bed the ground,
Which make a crunching, rustling sound.
Out come winter coats, scarfs and hats
And we look forward to Christmas, a time to relax.
The air is fresh, crisp and cold
And for bonfire night fireworks are sold.
But before the bonfires can be lit,
We must make the fire on which Guy Fawkes will sit.
Autumn is a great time of year,
So get out there!
And enjoy the season's good cheer.

Jenny Beard (11)
St Aidan's Technology College, Poulton Le Fylde

A GHOSTLY POEM

Frankenstein ate the witch
And the ghost dined on Frankenstein
The mummy gulped the ghost down
In scarcely any time.

Dracula chewed the mummy
But in hardly half a second
He was swallowed by the monster
Who was eaten by the phantom.

The phantom was rather careless
Who was gobbled to the bone
By an enterprising devil
Who fell victim to the clone.

The floath who fed upon the clone
Soon met another floath
And whilst they wondered what to do
The spider ate them both.

Cheryl Gourley (13)
St Aidan's Technology College, Poulton Le Fylde

THE MATCH

As we travelled to the match,
We talked about what the result
Might be, with hopes high and great expectations,
We queue outside the ground, with
Fans a-buzz of the latest signing.

As the match gets under way
We all start to sing and have our say,
To and fro the action goes
Being orchestrated by the referee's whistle.

It's half time there is no score,
We sit with our tea sorting out what
Will be in the second half.

Out they come after the break,
All to play for with lots at stake,
Suddenly the goal is scored,
But it's in the wrong net with not long to go,
We try our best but it's not to be,
We've lost again, we're bottom of Division 3.

Gary Creer (11)
St Aidan's Technology College, Poulton Le Fylde

ODE TO STARDOM

Oh somebody read this,
An agent or scout
In my bid for stardom
Please help me out.

I can warble light opera
And dance some spot tap
Play flute and piano
I've even tried rap.

I can belt out a show tune
Recite you a rhyme
Amaze you with Shakespeare
And mime you a mime.

No script is too small
I'll try them all now
A heroine, villain
Or a pantomime cow!

So Mr Director
I'm begging you please
I'll pose for the camera,
Smile and say cheese.

I can throw a good tantrum,
Scream, cry and shout
Just give me that break
And please help me out!

Rebecca Cutting (12)
St Aidan's Technology College, Poulton Le Fylde

LOOKING AT PHOTOGRAPHS

Joe, Jude and Jodie,
Me, Kieran and Mum,
Sitting on a high ledge,
Having some fun.

The edge of the world,
The desert in Saudi,
Is where I spent,
My last Friday.

We climbed the rocks
And took in the view,
Although we've been before,
It was breathtaking and new.

My dad and Kris,
Were there too,
Setting up the barbecue,
With lots to eat for us few.

We watched the sun
As it set with a glow,
Then we all packed up,
It was time to go.

I will always remember,
This special day,
As we are back here
And my friends are far away.

Dominique Holt (11)
St Aidan's Technology College, Poulton Le Fylde

BONFIRE NIGHT

Everyone gathers round the fire.
Whole sky lights up as fireworks go 'bang'
Smell of smoke from fire
Hear the fireworks?
'Bang'

It is cold, bonfire night,
Leaves fall to the floor.
Conkers on the grass.
Toffee apples and treacle toffee,
'Yum yum!'
Hear the fireworks?
'Bang'

Hear the crackling from the fire,
Hot on my face,
The Catherine wheel going round,
Making lovely colours in the sky.
Hear the fireworks?
'Bang'.

Hollie Jenkinson (12)
St Aidan's Technology College, Poulton Le Fylde

MY POEM

I like badminton
It's one of my favourite sports,
Especially when you play it,
On one of the courts.

I like football
If I can kick it hard,
It is such a popular sport,
You even find it on a birthday card.

I like all the sports
That you can name,
Not individual ones,
But team games.

Katie Fenton (11)
St Aidan's Technology College, Poulton Le Fylde

BONFIRE NIGHT

The bonfire crackling
In the night,
The firework's banging
In the night.

The treacle toffee crunching
In the night,
The toffee apples cracking
In the night.

The sparkler's crackling
In the night,
The leaves crunching
In the night.

The people laughing
In the night,
The babies crying
In the night.

All listening to the fireworks
Going bang, bang, bang
And watching the fire
Going crackle, crackle, crackle.

Paul Jenkinson (12)
St Aidan's Technology College, Poulton Le Fylde

AUTUMN POEM

The leaves are like breaking prawn crackers all shrivelled up and dry,
The leaves are all saying 'bye' to the tree, they used to live with,
The air is crisp and the soil soft and crumbly,
The earth's starting to get cooler, day by day, the wind's starting
To howl like mad wolves,
The noises of tractors in the field are like a roaring lion
That has just caught its prey,
The children down the street laugh like hyenas, very joyfully,
The taste of toffee apples all sticky in your hair,
That looks like a ball of red syrup.
The feel of berries in your head, exploding like a
Bomb of red and purple juice,
The leaves have fallen on the ground and now
They are fully brown and yellow.

It has arrived.

Amie Norris (11)
St Aidan's Technology College, Poulton Le Fylde

HOBBIES

Fishing,
Camping,
Playing tennis,
These are the things I like to do.
Night or day
It makes no difference.
In rain or hail
And sunshine too.
These are the things I like to do.

Dean Anderson (11)
St Aidan's Technology College, Poulton Le Fylde

AUTUMN

Autumn is the time of year when
Leaves drift lazily down.
They are as red as roses, as yellow as the sun
And as brown as wood.
I can hear the leaves crunching when
Someone stands on them, like when
You screw up a piece of paper.
Autumn brings bonfire night with fireworks
Like screaming kids and gunshots.
Colourful sparks fly from Catherine wheels and rockets.
You can eat toffee apples, treacle toffee
And baked potatoes.
The smell of fire lingers until the farmer
Comes with his tractor and muck spreader.
The red berries glow brightly against their
Green background.
Chill winds send animals scurrying to their
Beds to sleep through the long cold winter.

Nicola Entwisle (12)
St Aidan's Technology College, Poulton Le Fylde

FOOTBALL

F   is for fantastic and fouling,
O   is for offside and opposition,
O   is for overhead kicks,
T   is for tackling,
B   is for battling in the centre,
A   is for agility with the ball,
L   is for long distance shooting,
L   is for the left winger who crosses all the balls.

Ashlei Hodgson (11)
St Aidan's Technology College, Poulton Le Fylde

I Am Very Bothered When . . .

I am very bothered when I think,
Of the brilliant experiences I have had in my life.
Not least the time in primary school,
When I was in the running race
On sports day,
The crowds of people, the firing gun;
The race was off.

Oh the stretch of my legs,
As I made my way down
The track,
I was ahead of the other boys,
The anticipation of winning,
Was kicking in.

Please! I would give anything, if
Just to win this one race,
The finish line beckoned, and
I snatched the red tape.

James Cornall (15)
St Aidan's Technology College, Poulton Le Fylde

Autumn Time

It is a cool, crisp night
The birds are in flight,
It is a cool, crisp night
The leaves are a sight.

It is autumn time
Everything is fine
It is autumn time
The trees are out of prime.

Autumn's over
It is starting to snow
Autumn's over
It is time for it to go.

Winter has started
Autumn has parted
Winter has started
Autumn has gone.

Robert Meekins (13)
St Aidan's Technology College, Poulton Le Fylde

AUTUMN

Red, yellow, orange, brown,
The leaves of autumn all fall down
I can hear the crackling of the fireworks
And the bonfire burning!

The leaves in piles up to the sky
And the leaves are crispy dry,
The toffee apples are as red as berries
And the trees blowing in the breeze.

The wind blows a mighty gale
The squirrels with their big bushy tails,
Gather up nuts for winter
And the leaves blowing all directions.

The taste of toffee apples is delicious!
Some people are superstitious
Because of Guy Fawkes
Painful death!

Jennifer Smith (11)
St Aidan's Technology College, Poulton Le Fylde

HALLOWE'EN POEM

Trick or treat, trick or treat,
Give us something good to eat.

If it's bad, throw it in the bin, so
Trick or treat, trick or treat,
You better have something
Good to eat.

So here you go children 'No!'
This is bad we want
Something good to eat.

I have loads of good food
But I think you are a bit rude.

No we are not, you are
And we are going next door.

Lee Creer (12)
St Aidan's Technology College, Poulton Le Fylde

AUTUMN

Out in the autumn breeze
Something emerged from the trees,
It was dark at night,
Out shot a spray of light,
Next came the smoke,
Which caused me to choke,
I love toffee apples in the autumn
Also love running into the enormous
Piles of leaves,
I hate the smell of slurry
It makes me hurry.

James Wiseman (12)
St Aidan's Technology College, Poulton Le Fylde

LOOKING AT OLD PHOTOGRAPHS -
YUM, YUM, YUM CHOCOLATE IN MY TUM

Yum, yum, yum,
Chocolate in my tum,
Chocolate on the floor
And chocolate on the door.

Yum, yum, yum,
Chocolate in my tum,
Chocolate on my chair
And in my messy hair.

Yum, yum, yum,
Chocolate in my tum,
Chocolate on the wall
And on my uncle Paul.

Yum, yum, yum,
Chocolate in my tum,
Chocolate on my shirt
And chocolate on Mum's skirt.

Yum, yum, yum,
Chocolate in my tum,
Chocolate on the stair
And on my teddy bear.

Yum, yum, yum,
Chocolate in my tum,
Chocolate in the kitchen,
Chocolate's everywhere!

Joe Kelly (11)
St Aidan's Technology College, Poulton Le Fylde

THE WITCHES OF HALLOWE'EN

We are the witches of Hallowe'en,
The ugliest things you've ever seen,
We come out at night
And give you a fright,
We are the witches of Hallowe'en.

To people's houses in the night,
We fly on our broomsticks as fast as light,
We leave them outside,
We are coming in so you better hide,
We are the witches of Hallowe'en.

On our brooms and up into the air,
To give more people a horrible scare.
Over the hills and into the cities,
Petting and stroking our black kitties,
We are the witches of Hallowe'en.

Late at night into our pj's and off with our sandals,
Tucked into bed and blow out the candles,
So pleasant dreams and sleep tight
And make sure that the 'deadbugs' don't bite.
We are the witches of Hallowe'en.

Daniel Harrison (11)
St Aidan's Technology College, Poulton Le Fylde

LOOKING AT THE PHOTOGRAPHS

It was a wet rainy day,
Our cousins called Daniel and Richard came to stay,
What can we do they would say,
What can we play?
What can we play?

Paints and colour funny faces,
Take us to magical places,
Zig zags, harlequins and funny clowns,
Smiling happy faces all around.

Joanne Dolphin (11)
St Aidan's Technology College, Poulton Le Fylde

WOUNDED SOLDIERS

The skies are black and full of hate
I use to love a girl called Kate
Stuck in the trenches, people are scared
They sometimes call out but are not heard.

Guns at the ready and pointing to the sky
Wounded soldiers lie on the ground ready to die
People at wars' mercy and almost dead
People dying who have bled.

There is a sense of pain lurking all around
People at the front are falling to the ground
Grenades are flying through the air, striking with deadly aim
Soldiers look up and pray that it's all a game.

Soldiers are running trying to avoid being shot
Others aren't so lucky and are hit on the spot
Rain is falling and it is very wet
The enemy is very near but not close enough to get.

The soldiers are dying in their muddy pit
Even though they seemed so fit
They slowly close their eyes and drift away
And in peace, have nothing else to say.

Peter Robinson (14)
St Aidan's Technology College, Poulton Le Fylde

FOOD

Food, food is all over the place
Food, food is sometimes a waste,
It's in cans and cartons, trolleys and bags,
Some people take it in place of the fags.

Food can be cold,
Food can be hot,
Taken at times when you think not.

Vegetables and greens are good for you,
But veg can taste like elephant stew.
Sweets are not but what the eek
Take them when you feel the peck.

The food at school is more than I can eat,
Dinnertime comes, it's such a treat,
Waste not, want not, I hear you say,
The only problem is I have to pay.

Adam Harwood (11)
St Aidan's Technology College, Poulton Le Fylde

FOOTBALL WITH PAUL

All year round I like to play football,
I play with my next door neighbour Paul.
We especially like to play in the rain,
I am destined for football fame.

He always wins and I get mucky,
He only wins because he is lucky.
After that he goes for tea,
Then he comes back to play with me.

Paul is my friend because he is cool,
He also has a swimming pool.
He's a really good friend to me,
He's the kind of person I want to be.

I want to be like Paul because he is funny,
He also has a lot of money,
He is generous, he is kind,
If you call him a name he won't mind.

Chris Curwen (13)
St Aidan's Technology College, Poulton Le Fylde

FOOTBALL IS A GAME OF TWO HALVES

Football is a game of two halves,
Beckham, Ronaldo, Zola, Bierhoff.
Champions League, FA Cup,
Those are the games that make me jump.

England are my national team,
All they do is make me scream.
When Germany scored their winning goal,
I wanted to bury myself in a hole.

When Man U won that amazing treble,
The people acted such rebels
When Ole put that great ball through.
I was sitting on the loo.

The header, the volley, the chip and kick,
That's what makes this game tick.
Win or lose I'll still cheer,
For the great teams of this era.

Peter Cox (13)
St Aidan's Technology College, Poulton Le Fylde

KUNG FU

Me and you can learn Kung Fu
It's very tricky and hard to do.
I could hit you and you could hit me
And maybe one day we'll be on TV.
Though your uniform is not pj's,
You can wear them for days and days,
You only wash it when it gets stiff
Or maybe when it starts to whiff.
I'd like to tell you and make you a bet
That you couldn't do it without breaking a sweat,
So one of these days you'd better beware
In case I creep up on you and give you a scare.

Chris Marsters (11)
St Aidan's Technology College, Poulton Le Fylde

CHARACTERS

Characters, characters,
Happy, sad and crazy,
Sometimes full of life
And sometimes very lazy.

Characters, characters,
Say Chicken Run,
When have you ever had
So much fun?

Characters, characters,
Say Winnie the Pooh
Eeyore, Piglet
And Tigger too.

Lianne Camp (11)
St Aidan's Technology College, Poulton Le Fylde

198

MY NEXT DOOR NEIGHBOURS

Guess who I live next door to?
No, you'd never guess! Well, I'll tell you.
I live next door to a bunch of . . .
Ah! Yes, I've remembered now!

Of Zombies and ghouls and ghosties galore,
Of demons and vampires and plenty things more,
There's skeletons and devils and heaven knows what,
There's witches and wizards and oh! What a lot!

I can see that you're wondering where they all live,
I guess you didn't know I live next door to a spooky graveyard
And that's where they live!
But Mum and Dad, they look dreadfully pale
And now they're putting our house up for sale!

Zoë Christoforou (12)
St Aidan's Technology College, Poulton Le Fylde

AUTUMN

Autumn leaves brown and dry,
The air smells like apple pie,
Children watch the fireworks,
When parents come home from a hard day's work.

Frosty mornings, dark nights,
Children are having conker fights,
Fireworks set off like rockets,
While children put conkers in their pockets.

I hope you have enjoyed my rhyme
And have a very nice autumn time.

Mark Ruthven (11)
St Aidan's Technology College, Poulton Le Fylde

AUTUMN POEM

Fireworks sparkling everywhere look like shooting stars
Up in the air, Catherine wheels swimming like eels in the
Black sky.
October is approaching, it's time for Hallowe'en so get
Out your masks because it's time to let out a scream.
Autumn is the time when colours start to shine.
Leaves fall off the trees like floating feathers in the breeze.
Lots of leaves fall on the ground and there are lots of
Colours to be found.
All the woodland animals scurrying around collecting
Their precious
Food from the ground.
Kestrels hovering in the air give the mice a little scare.

Rebecca Finlay (11)
St Aidan's Technology College, Poulton Le Fylde

I AM NOT VERY BOTHERED . . .

I am not very bothered when I talk
Of bad things I have done in my life.
Not at least that time when I pushed the
Vase off the table and ran off quick.

Oh the great feeling of shifting the blame
As the dreaded brother of mine was caught
By mother while he was picking up my pieces
Damaged my mother said.
Damaged by eternity.

Don't believe me please if I say it was just
My elbow that got in my way.

Adam Spedding (15)
St Aidan's Technology College, Poulton Le Fylde

AUTUMN

Autumn is many things
Fireworks pop in the sky like a gun
Leaves fall from the trees one by one,
That's what makes it such fun.

Autumn is many things
Treacle toffee, toffee apples too,
Goodies that stick to your teeth like glue
I love the tastes, it is true.

Autumn is many things
Trickers and treaters are often seen,
Kids in fancy dress at Hallowe'en
The trees are no longer green.

Jack Hayhurst (12)
St Aidan's Technology College, Poulton Le Fylde

SENSES OF AUTUMN

Conkers spike my fingers,
They feel like hedgehogs backs,
A colourful rainbow in the sky,
Is a million butterflies,
Waterfalls like God moving his furniture
And never making his mind up,
Grandma's apple pie,
Tastes like a thousand orchards -
A blanket of fruit,
The smell of newly baked bread,
Fresh from the oven.

Sasha Maughan (11)
St Aidan's Technology College, Poulton Le Fylde

AUTUMN POEM

Autumn is a very colourful season,
Leaves all different shades of crimson,
They fall like a blanket of fire on the ground,
With the wind blowing them all around.

The farmers are gathering their crops
And geese are flying in noisy flocks,
Harvest festivals are being held,
Apples are being caramelled.

In preparation for bonfire night,
Bang! Whoosh! Crash! Wee!
Rockets in flight,
I think treacle toffee,
Is a lot better than banoffee.

Alexandra Pickersgill (11)
St Aidan's Technology College, Poulton Le Fylde

AUTUMN

Fireworks are like stars that burst,
Like a handful of popcorn popping in the sky,
At Hallowe'en there's cackling by little girls,
Dressed like witches.
There are leaves dry and crisp or wet and soggy,
The fireworks sound like screams and bombs
And the colours are golden brown, fiery reds,
Browny oranges.
Autumn is a time of love and laughter,
It brings people together
And joins people's hearts.

Laurie Dickson-Smith (11)
St Aidan's Technology College, Poulton Le Fylde

AUTUMN POEM

The golden leaves falling off the blowing trees,
Fireworks going up as elephants feet banging on the ground,
The taste of the big sticky toffee apples crunching in our mouth,
The big pile of leaves dancing as a gang of girls,
The touch of the cricket bark on the trees, big and brown
Like orangey and bright yellowy fire burning away,
The wind screaming as a recorder playing,
The smell of cow muck spreading around the fields,
The big berries red as a clown's nose,
The rain falling down as a waterfall,
Legs and arms no longer bare now covered in
Woolly jumpers of fur.

Lisa Belsey (11)
St Aidan's Technology College, Poulton Le Fylde

AUTUMN POEM

The leaves are red, brown and golden,
The autumn gales blow them off the trees,
The fireworks go whoosh and bang and sound
Like screaming girls,
They light up the sky with rainbow colours,
The smell of fireworks and bonfires fills the air,
The cold wind makes my nose tingle,
The toffee apples taste sweet and are crunchy,
Hallowe'en is scaring down my street,
All you hear is screaming,
All you see are ghosts, vampires and ghouls.

Ben Taylor (11)
St Aidan's Technology College, Poulton Le Fylde

LITTLE SISTERS - LOOKING AT OLD PHOTOGRAPHS

I do hate little sisters,
One I know is immature,
She dances on the floor,
She thinks she's at a ball.

She likes to be in charge,
But she's only very small,
She dresses up at night
And often gives me a fright.

I would hate to be a girl,
Especially one like that,
I don't know why they do this,
Maybe it's just an act.

J Robinson (11)
St Aidan's Technology College, Poulton Le Fylde

AUTUMN POEM

Autumn leaves are blowing around,
Rustling, rustling, making a lovely sound.
The wind around us groans and howls,
Making a sound of ghostly owls.
Different coloured leaves I can now see,
Red, brown and yellow, all from one tree.
Fireworks we watch around a fire bright,
They burst through the sky for everyone's delight.
Lots of lovely smells are all around,
Toffee apples and jacket potatoes all for a pound.

Matthew Humphrey (11)
St Aidan's Technology College, Poulton Le Fylde

AUTUMN

In autumn when the leaves blow by
And the fireworks shoot up into the sky
And when you're eating toffee apples all night long
And when the wind is howling fierce and strong.

When the trees turn brown, the time has come,
To trick or treat, it's lots of fun,
When the moon is up and the stars are high,
Beware of the witches flying by.

If you like the autumn, with its cooling breeze
And you really don't mind the odd cough or sneeze,
Now autumn has run aground
And now it's time for winter to be crowned . . .

Michael Willacy (11)
St Aidan's Technology College, Poulton Le Fylde

AUTUMN POEM

The bonfire goes up with a mighty roar
And everyone waves their sparklers
When everyone counts down to the rocket,
It feels like a new year.

When the leaves fall off the trees,
They are gold and brown and red,
It's just like me getting up in the morning
And falling back onto my bed.

The smell of the air is refreshing
And other people think that too,
Because it's the start of the new millennium,
Everything is new!

Scott Coultas (11)
St Aidan's Technology College, Poulton Le Fylde

FLEETWOOD FALL

As I awoke from my sleep I fell downstairs in a big heap!
At the bottom step of the hall, went for breakfast to find nothing at all,
Felt the chill of the autumn frost, goodness me I feel lost
Woolly hats, cosy gloves for the air outside is full of frost
Slippy paths that I might slide, on my way to the Memorial Park
Leaves that have turned golden brown, now lay upon the ground
Over there chestnut trees only to find squirrels up a tree
Underneath scurrying through horse chestnut for me and you
Fir cones rest on the floor waiting for children to gather more
Then a rustle and a shower of the leaves that are falling down
As I looked all around everything seems to be turning golden brown
Many summer flowers are now gone, hawthorn berries in the sun
Hedgerows season of mist in our amethyst
All Gods creatures gone to sleep, shhh not a peak.

Emma Sessions (13)
St Aidan's Technology College, Poulton Le Fylde

AUTUMN

Russet, ochre, dappled leaves,
Falling, swirling, cascading to the ground,
Mother Nature silently waits to receive
Her offspring with open arms safe and sound.

Shy creatures of the forest live in fear,
Squirrels hiding food - hiding in the trees,
Watching for trespassing humans to appear,
Longing not to be found, longing for some peace.

Children trick or treating, playing nasty games,
Dancing with the devil - hiding behind a mask,
Witches, ghouls and vampires are all evil names,
Hallowe'en is such a devilish task.

Popping, whizzing what a spectacular sight,
Banging, frapping, fizzing fireworks in the sky,
Dogs howling, babies bawling in the night,
Celebrating treason - I wonder why?

Adéle Jenkinson (11)
St Aidan's Technology College, Poulton Le Fylde

AUTUMN POEM

Leaves are falling, flowers die.
How the summer days have passed us by.
Leaves are brown, flowers are leaning
Christmas lights display their meaning.

Bonfires, bonfires everywhere.
You can even smell them in the air.
Fireworks banging, children shouting.
Lots of fume and black smoke about.

Birds migrating to warm climates.
Animals hibernating for winter nights.
Now they are dreaming of warmer days.
Looking forward to the sun's rays.

Autumn days are here again.
Long winter days are damp and cold.
School seems even longer these days.
How I dream of school holidays.

Rachel Spurgeon (13)
St Aidan's Technology College, Poulton Le Fylde

LOOKING AT THE OLD PHOTOS

I remember when
I was six years old,
It was a nice day but a little cold,
I was riding round on my bike,
On the back lawn,
My brother Robert was lying in the middle,
As I rode around, I started to giggle,
Robert started laughing his head off
And I fell off,
My seat spun round
And I hit my head on the ground,
My head started to bleed,
We shouted for Rita next door,
Who had seen me laying on the floor,
She looked at the wound
And dealt with it.

Laura Singleton (11)
St Aidan's Technology College, Poulton Le Fylde

LOOKING AT OLD PHOTOGRAPHS

Oh you should have seen the grin on his face,
It was a big cheeky grin.
I was furious,
I had just sorted out my ribbons and bobbles
And what had he done?
Scattered them all over the floor,
Then sat in the drawer.
My one year old mischievous brother!
But I couldn't be mad for long because I loved him.
In a way it was very funny,
Him and his cheeky grin.

Mandy Swarbrick (11)
St Aidan's Technology College, Poulton Le Fylde

AUTUMN POEM

Autumn leaves fall to the ground,
Hush! They make no sound.
Crunchy and crisp, rusty brown and blood red,
From the big oak tree they fall, dead!
When you step the leaves scrunch and crunch,
Leaving leaves all in a bunch.

Then after that comes Hallowe'en,
Dark nights and spooky scenes.
Pumpkins like shining faces,
All lit up on the window in their places.
Makes me smile when I see them,
Like faces looking at me when I see them.

Bonfire night is not far from that,
The fire is fruit orange, blood red and things like that.
This is like a great big ball of fire,
That makes you wonder if it could roll like a tyre.
The fireworks are spectacular,
In raindrops and rainbows that light up in the special sky.

Natalie Harrison (13)
St Aidan's Technology College, Poulton Le Fylde

AUTUMN

Like rusty red rivers rolling round the street,
I can hear the crunching under my feet,
The dew on the leaves and the frost in the trees,
Sends a cold shiver into my knees.
The banging at night means it's bonfire night,
The thumping at the door means treats are in store for all
The trick or treaters behind the closed door.

Louise Rhodes (13)
St Aidan's Technology College, Poulton Le Fylde

THE SOUND OF AUTUMN

I like the sound of
The wind as it
Whistles through
The trees like a
Soft voice.

I like the sound of
The brown crisp
Leaves as they
Crunch beneath
My feet.

I like the sound of
The fireworks on
Bonfire night as they
Crack and bang
And whistle through
The air with a boom!

Abra Speakmen (14)
St Aidan's Technology College, Poulton Le Fylde

LOOKING AT OLD PHOTOGRAPHS

My brother playing football,
On a Sunday afternoon
In the cold and rain,
Playing on a muddy field,
My brother scores a goal,
To the cheering crowd
Yes another win on a wet afternoon
My brother's a hero in the changing room.

John Cummings (11)
St Aidan's Technology College, Poulton Le Fylde

BRUNO V'S HOLLYFIELD

Ding, ding, the match is underway
And both of the fighters plan to stay.
They dance around looking for a chance
To fire in a left hook or a right glance.

Bruno jabs and releases a big one,
Hollyfield dodges like an elegant swan.
He tries the famous English uppercut,
But Bruno blocks it, the door slams shut.

The American crowd is most partisan,
They scream and shout as loud as they can.
Bruno puts fear into all the home nation
By giving Evander a head laceration.

The ref calls a halt to the fight,
The American's face is a bloody sight,
After the medic has taken a look,
There is more facial damage with a Bruno left hook.

At the end of round five the corner works hard
And Evander's face is smothered in lard.
The boxers are tired, the next round seems slow,
Then Bruno's knocked down with a very low blow.

The referee announces the disqualification
To the dismay of the American nation.
Bruno's the champ, the Brit has prevailed,
Poor old Evander has cheated and failed.

Matt Horton (13)
St Aidan's Technology College, Poulton Le Fylde

BLOOD ON HIS HANDS

Blood on his hands,
Like scarlet gloves
Skin tight and damp,
Warm to the touch
Yet heart-stoppingly cold.

Blood on his hands
Held aloft like a trophy,
The prize of war
Bloodshed
Life lost.

Slumped on the street
Lifeless and pale,
The ruby tide recedes
And life ebbs away,
His blood on someone else's hands.

When war is over
And all fights are done,
Crimson stains
Tell everyone there is
Blood on both their hands.

Harry Morgan (14)
St Aidan's Technology College, Poulton Le Fylde

MY DRESS

All the presents I could see,
My face was happy filled with glee.
Here it was, the last of them all
It was squeegee and was quite small.
I opened it up only to see,
A waistcoat and dress that went down to my knee.
I did not like it one little bit
I tried it on but it wouldn't fit.

My mum and dad said 'Doesn't it look nice?'
But I replied 'You better think twice.'
The next day came, the worst day of all
Nanna with her camera
Taking pictures in the hall.
I had to wear my dress, life wasn't fair
And now my picture will be hung everywhere.

Leanna Elliott (11)
St Aidan's Technology College, Poulton Le Fylde

HEIDI

I have a dog, her name is Heidi-Ho,
She stinks of old dead fish
But oh I love her so!

She bites my fingers
And scratches my legs,
But she's the cutest thing on four legs!

She begs for food
And shows you puppy eyes,
Sometimes she moans and cries!

She has big floppy ears
And gorgeous black fur
And a little wet nose
Oh and she hates the hose!

She is scared of Hoovers
And hairdryers
And water too.
In fact I think the only thing
She's not scared of is food!

Carla Savage
St Aidan's Technology College, Poulton Le Fylde

LOOKING AT OLD PHOTOGRAPHS

There were two of us in our house,
One big, one small,
One of us used to play with building bricks
And one of us with a ball.

Best friends we were at one time,
When we played in mum's hall.

Then we both grew up and one was really tall,
My brother he was boss,
Making me feel small,
But we're still friends big or small,
Sharing laughs and hobbies galore.

Luke Robert Yates (11)
St Aidan's Technology College, Poulton Le Fylde

LOOKING AT OLD PHOTOGRAPHS

Here we are one, two, three,
Dressed up my brother, my dad and me,
Christmas is nearly here,
Can you see the tree?

Here we are one, two, three,
Wearing our ties, my brother and me,
Dad in his waistcoat, look and see,
Can you guess it's Christmas Eve!

Here we are one, two, three,
Laughing and smiling and ready for tea,
Christmas tomorrow, let's wait and see
What Father Christmas is bringing for me!

Adam Turner (11)
St Aidan's Technology College, Poulton Le Fylde

HOME AT NOON

Trench spirit is high
We've said our goodbye's,
We're all very happy, do you know why?
We're all going home at noon.

My head is still banging from the previous night,
Most of our ammo was set alight,
But what does it matter to me now?
I'm going home at noon.

The war no longer seems negative.
I've alerted my relatives,
I've packed my bag and lowered the flag
And I'm coming home at noon.

The trenches are cleared, some soldiers shed tears,
Many served here for years.
Nothing bothers me, we all know why,
I'm going home at noon.

We begin to march, I'm starting to parch,
It has been a long campaign,
It's beginning to rain, I don't care,
Cos I'm going home at noon.

Mortars blast! We hit the ground,
I'm thinking we've been found.
The explosions get nearer,
But I'm going home at noon.

A bullet zips past my ear,
Here comes another, this won't miss.
It hits us dead on, my regiment has gone,
I'm not going home at noon.

Paul Armer (13)
St Aidan's Technology College, Poulton Le Fylde

THE BEST CHRISTMAS EVER!

As I awoke on Christmas morning,
I scratched my head, I couldn't stop yawning.

I crept downstairs to fetch my mum,
To see if the man in red had come.

She said, 'Hang on a minute while I'll go and see,'
If there's been anything left for me.

'OK come in' to my delight,
The man in red had been busy here all night.

I took a deep breath, I just couldn't,
All this was for me it was hard to believe.

There were lots of boxes, things of all shapes,
Beautifully wrapped parcels and a large Christmas cake.

I started to unwrap with no hesitation,
I couldn't believe it! I had a PlayStation.

Lots of nice clothes and a lovely gold ring,
All the things that I dreamed of I'd got everything.

A metal detector, a pair of black boots,
A glittery dress and a shiny gold suit.

A set of great make-up and things for my hair,
A pair of pjyamas and a cuddly bear.

I gave out my presents for my dad and my mum,
Some toys for my brother so that he could have fun.

I got out a bin bag and picked up my wrapping,
I could hear a loud noise, it was some kind of tapping.

It was coming from outside so I thought in my head,
I think I'll investigate this noise in our shed.

So I opened the shed door and there to my shock,
There was a big purple bike, a helmet and a bike lock.

Oh what a day that I have had,
The best mum in the world, best brother and best dad.

Stacey McClean (11)
St Aidan's Technology College, Poulton Le Fylde

MY AUTUMN POEM

When you open the door in the morning,
The lovely fresh air bursts in like a rocket
And fills the dark but small room.
You can smell the burning of the bonfire,
If you step too close it burns you like the sun
On a roasting summer's day.

The colours of the leaves like a technicoloured dream coat,
They rustle when the wind rushes through them
And they crunch like a crisp packet
As you step on them.

On bonfire night you taste the
Warm, smooth, golden toffee, trickling through your teeth,
Like water in a river
And the warm, tasty hot pot,
Like a hot, exotic country.

Lauren Gardner (13)
St Aidan's Technology College, Poulton Le Fylde

A Flash In A Woman's Life

Stars of yellow strike as a beginning of a dream,
Minds fill with love, joy, peace and hate.
Hearts pump in a fierce heart rate.

Clothes cover a naked eye with judgement does the spy,
Spy of human nature fall down to his grave
Or does he enjoy love, others hate?

Choices, choices does power have hope?
I think he's getting to our lives so we don't cope.

He has taken your heart from all feeling inside.
It's time to let yourself forgive him.
It's time to start a new star of pride.

Christine Dolphin (15)
St Aidan's Technology College, Poulton Le Fylde

Autumn

Shooting up like shooting stars,
Rockets! Rockets! Everywhere,
Sparkling, fizzing like a fire.
Crunch go the leaves like children
Eating crunchy crisps.
Bright lights! They come and go
In the dark sky,
Who wants chocolate and chocolate apples,
'Me! Me!' Shout the children.
I think the best part of autumn is
The different colours.

Rebecca Jackson (12)
St Aidan's Technology College, Poulton Le Fylde

SMUGGLERS

What's that?
'Crash, bang!'
A faint noise woke the night.
I ran to the window,
And slowly, I drew the curtains.

I could not describe
What I saw through my eyes.
The village was alive, at night?
Boxes around.
Banging away, the villagers worked.

I thought it was a dream,
But then bright lights shone at me!
They were looking at me!
Horror struck,
They all stopped!

I quickly ran to my bed,
Covers over me,
I had to know,
I just had to know what they were doing,
But it could wait until morning!

Early morning, I wake up,
Everything quiet,
No one stirring!
I crept into my mother's bedroom,
Blood and glass lay everywhere!

Graham Harwood (13)
St Aidan's Technology College, Poulton Le Fylde

THE WORLD

The world is one great ocean,
Freckled by spots of land,
To outsiders (or aliens)
It must seem very grand,
Compared to Mars
Vast, red and dry,
Or maybe even Mercury,
Where I would surely fry
And compared to Jupiter,
With its great big spot on the chin
And life on the moon,
Would surely create a din!
But Earth has one tiny flaw,
Disease, destruction, poverty and war,
Has torn the world apart in two
And no thanks to me nor you.
The nations are divided -
And there they will stay,
Until people such as Princess Diana and Nelson Mandela,
Have had their say,
For then the world will be a happy place,
United every religion and race.

Erin Basey (11)
St Aidan's Technology College, Poulton Le Fylde

TRICK OR TREAT

Trick or treat, trick or treat,
The children shout to me.
The noises of the street make
Me want to scream.

Trick or treat, trick or treat,
The children shout again.
I put sweets into the bag
And say please don't call again.

Averil Christopher (14)
St Aidan's Technology College, Poulton Le Fylde

SMUGGLERS

I looked through the window,
For the very first time.
All was still,
Even the old mill.
But wait, what's that?
A man out at this time,
Moving through the pines.
They are climbing the hill,
Wait, they are talking to Bill.
They are carrying barrels,
And singing carols,
While breathing in the nightly air.

I hear horses,
Trotting through the woods,
All of the men,
Hiding under hoods.
Maybe I should
Look away.
I hear footsteps,
Coming up the stairs,
I'll get back into bed,

And never breathe a word,
Of this to anyone!

Rachel Morris (13)
St Aidan's Technology College, Poulton Le Fylde

AUTUMN

I can see the falling of the leaves,
They fall off the big stumpy trees.
I can see the blood red, the sunlight orange
Rusty brown and the fire yellow.

The sound of the fireworks make me jump,
As they shoot in the sky in a big round clump.
I see a deep scarlet, dazzling purple
And one that even looks like a turtle.

The burning of the bonfire is like the heat from the sun,
Then the fireworks sound again,
I'm having so much fun.

Becky Bairstow (13)
St Aidan's Technology College, Poulton Le Fylde

AUTUMN

Autumn is a funny season
As the nights draw in
And the weather cools down
Seeing the people begin to frown.

Autumn's when it's cold and wet
But something's are fun, so hey don't fret!

There's Hallowe'en or 'trick or treat'
Where you go out
And get tons of sweets.

Bonfire night, that's really cool
Seeing the sky light up with
Different coloured balls.

Emma Morley (13)
St Aidan's Technology College, Poulton Le Fylde

A POEM ABOUT FLOWERS

Flowers smell nice,
Flowers look pretty,
Flowers can be any colour really.
Red,
Green,
Yellow,
Blue,
Yes! That's it, they will do.
Flowers of different shapes and sizes
Round, oval, even spiky,
Big ones, small ones,
Tall ones too,
Oh! Those are lovely, go on I'll have two.

Laura Fishwick (13)
St Aidan's Technology College, Poulton Le Fylde

DON'T MENTION DETENTION!

It's the gravitational field strength I'm told,
I can't understand, I'm too tired and cold.
Will we ever need to know this again?
To me, it's just one huge pain!
Why can't I be doing something more fun?
Like going for a run or baking a bun.
Suddenly I start daydreaming,
To be woken up by the teacher screaming.
Why, oh why is it always me?
I was only wondering, 'What's for tea?'
I try again to pay attention,
Only to be told, 'You've got detention!'

Dawn Bottomley (15)
St Aidan's Technology College, Poulton Le Fylde

AUTUMN DAYS

The darkness of the sky closes in as the
Light fades, while night draws in.
The leaves crunch as people walk by,
The rusty colours and the scarlet reds
Remind me of the autumn sky.

The streets deserted as the wind grows sharper,
The trees lose their leaves as they rustle on by,
As morning returns and darkness fades,
The shiny dew sparkles against the grass.

A cool fresh morning begins the day,
A light mist beams down from the big, bright sun,
At first dawn, the light breaks through
And as the sun shines filters over the land
It seeps through the curtains and is
Ready to greet you as you wake.

Vicky Guest (13)
St Aidan's Technology College, Poulton Le Fylde

LOOKING THROUGH THE BABY BOOK

Looking through the baby book
It made me have a real good look.
The pictures in the book did show
I'm destined to be in the know!
One of the pictures stood out
Where I'm giving a pair of glasses a clout,
For one of the Blues Brothers I'm meant to be,
As you obviously can see
I will entertain anywhere,
Even with no underwear.

Alex Allen (12)
St Aidan's Technology College, Poulton Le Fylde

SMUGGLING

A noise coming from outside,
Looking through my window,
I couldn't believe my eyes.
People pushing barrels down the street,
Wondering what they're doing scuffling their feet.
Not got a clue what they're doing.
Or what they were moving.
Barrels came from a boat,
So I picked up my coat,
And wandered outside.
I'm wanting to know what they're doing,
Outside all to-ing and fro-ing.
I decided I'd go ask my dad,
If what he was going was good or bad.
He said, 'Don't worry love, it's ok,
It's only for a day.'
'What is it?'
'What's it called?'
'Just be quiet.' My father bawled!
I ran upstairs, lay on my bed,
With everything still going through my head,
Then I realised what it was.
This smuggling I'd been once told of.
Yes that's it!
Smuggling.

Natalie Coleman (12)
St Aidan's Technology College, Poulton Le Fylde

SMUGGLERS

I looked down to the road,
Through the vicious rain,
Splashing water off the cobble
Running down the drain.

The look of clouds above,
It's not looking nice,
There are people out there
On this dreadful night.

The people of the village,
Are all out there,
Running around with boxes
Here, there and everywhere.

The look on their faces,
Is that of dismay,
Wishing these clouds would pass
And the rain go away.

I ran down the stairs,
To help them as they go,
They will succeed with my help
Not lose with misery and woe.

Bradey Pogson (13)
St Aidan's Technology College, Poulton Le Fylde

AUTUMN

The smell of manure on the farm,
Is a sign for animals to set their alarm,
All the animals fall fast asleep,
Before the pile of leaves is too deep.

People play out in the rain,
But they get wet again and again,
People get out their woolly hats
And light the fire for the cat.

Iain Fenton (13)
St Aidan's Technology College, Poulton Le Fylde

PIRATES

I saw a ship coming towards me
As I climbed up the sea wall
As it drew nearer one of the crew members waved at me
He had a parrot, but it was only small.

The parrot was red, yellow, blue and green
It was as they got closer I realised
That the men were pirates
As some of them had black eye patches

Most had black hats with a skull and crossbone
One had a peg leg
But with a crutch under his left arm
He hopped along like a bird.

One of the pirates climbed to shore
And introduced himself as 'Pew'
The man with the peg leg
Introduced himself as Long John Silver.

We went for a walk along the quay
He told me some interesting things
I am going on a journey with them in five days
To find a loot of treasure.

Danielle Bamber (12)
St Aidan's Technology College, Poulton Le Fylde

PARTY FEVER!

Birthday parties, Christmas parties,
New Year parties too,
Easter parties, Hallowe'en parties,
One for me and for you,
To make the perfect party,
There's a lot to organise,
There's a fancy cake and music,
Not forgetting a party prize.

Party games and party gifts,
To make you feel alive,
So bang on the funky music
And get down here and jive,
But if dancing to the funky music,
Really ain't your style,
Maybe you should sing it,
With a karaoke smile.

Laura Sulley (13)
St Aidan's Technology College, Poulton Le Fylde

AUTUMN

Bang, bang, bang!
The fireworks go clang.
The fire goes whoosh,
The people go cold.
The children scream and shout,
Their parents give them a clout.
The toffee apples are eaten,
So the wind is beating.

Kirsty Rawlinson (13)
St Aidan's Technology College, Poulton Le Fylde

BILLY THE OUTSIDER

There was a boy called Billy
Who had no friends,
They all called him Billy no-mates,
Which made him upset.

When he got home
He told his mum about them,
'Those boys are calling me names,
Whatever shall I do?'

His mum went to school about it,
She told the head about them,
'They are calling my son names,
Whatever shall we do?'

The bullies realised how cruel they had been
And decided to make friends,
Billy was very pleased
That he was no longer Billy no-mates.

Sarah Ellis (12)
St Aidan's Technology College, Poulton Le Fylde

AUTUMN

A   ll the leaves fall off trees,
U   mbrellas at the ready,
T   rees are bare,
U   mbrellas flying in the air,
M   ost animals migrate,
N   ow animals hibernate.

Stu Belsey
St Aidan's Technology College, Poulton Le Fylde

AUTUMN TIME

Autumn time you can have lots of fun.
Dancing, crunching on the leaves.
The only thing is there's no sun.
All of the leaves have fallen off the trees.

It's so cold,
So wrap up warm
Because it's cold out there.
You might get caught in a storm.

Bonfire night is finally here.
Snap, bang, crackle, pop.
Ow! It's hurting my eye,
But I never want it to stop.

Leanne Gillett (13)
St Aidan's Technology College, Poulton Le Fylde

IN AUTUMN

Leaves are falling
Cold is dawning.
Colours bright
In the night.

Witches and ghosts
Children make the most,
Cos next year
They may be too old to give fear.

Smell the fire, burning bright
See the fireworks bright light.
Catherine wheels spinning around
Wow, the rockets, what a sound!

Rosalyn Hodgson (13)
St Aidan's Technology College, Poulton Le Fylde

THE GOLFER

Each and every golfer who plays the game
Are nearly all the same.
There are ones that are good
Like everyone should.

Whoever hits the ball further than your eyes can see,
Then they are the ones that are not at all good.
Whoever keeps hitting the ball into the mud
These are people like you and me.

Then there are the ones that are bad
And hit it like they are mad,
These people are just like my dad.

Andrew Crossley
St Aidan's Technology College, Poulton Le Fylde

AUTUMN DAYS

Autumn days,
when the grass is green
and the leaves are orange, yellow and red.
The paths go crunch
as the leaves go scrunch,
when people stand on them.
The air is fresh
but the leaves are dead.
And there's lots of great things to do,
Hallowe'en and bonfire night
and toffee apples to chew.
Yes, there are many things to do.

Amy Parkes (13)
St Aidan's Technology College, Poulton Le Fylde

AUTUMN

Here is autumn once again,
I see the leaves falling
through the window pane,
as they drop it looks like it's raining.

Crunch, crunch, crunch,
go the leaves as I step on them,
we will be all drinking punch at
the Hallowe'en party.

Bang, bang, bang,
go the fireworks as they're let off.
See how they light the sky up,
hear how they whistle through
the sky.

Samantha Roskell (13)
St Aidan's Technology College, Poulton Le Fylde

AUTUMN LEAVES

A utumn leaves go golden brown,
U mbrellas are seen in town,
T rees start to bend and strain,
U nending queues in the pouring rain,
M other tucking us in at night,
N ights long and dark, lit with candle light.

Mark Berwick (13)
St Aidan's Technology College, Poulton Le Fylde

SMUGGLERS

I am walking down the road with my men,
I work for the king and so do all of them.
We can see and hear everything around,
Not even a mouse could make a sound.

What's that I see on the Cornish coastline,
The very men that we've been looking for all this time.
The smugglers there with their barrels
And their leader, old Jim Huckets.

They're walking away from some rowing boats,
Whistling their merry notes.
They're heading towards the hills but the British army
Will end their thrills and I will finally catch
Old Jim Huckets with his babble of men
And their barrels and buckets.

Ian Foster (12)
St Aidan's Technology College, Poulton Le Fylde

AUTUMN

A   ll the crunchy leaves fall off the trees,
U   mbrellas being used every day,
T   rees with no leaves left on them,
U   mbrellas being carried off by the wind,
M   igration, all the birds go to a warmer place,
N   ights are getting longer and colder.

Emma Ganderton (14)
St Aidan's Technology College, Poulton Le Fylde

WHY NOT INCLUDE ME

Why not include me,
Everyone else is doing it,
But what could it be,
I better go and see.

Why not include me,
There's people carrying barrels,
That's what I see,
Oh, why not include me.

I look out of the window,
All the adults are there,
Walking and walking very slow,
Walking quietly to and fro.

Why not include me,
There's people carrying barrels,
That's what I see,
Oh, why not include me.

I heard my father talking
About it to his friend,
Then I saw him walking,
This whole thing is smuggling.

Helen Lawrenson
St Aidan's Technology College, Poulton Le Fylde

SMUGGLERS

The moon ripples in the sea
A breeze passes by
Gentle drips of rain falls down
As I'm walking through town.

A whistle, yet no sound
Light flickers all around
A rustle, on the ground
Light flickers all around.

Smugglers here and there,
A town up a night
Still, light flickers all around.

Moving up close
Still no sound, closely, closely
Hush, no sound
But light flickers all around.

There they are, eight of them
Dare I question, dare I ask
Dare I tell?
No!
But the light flickers all around.

Thomas Jackson (13)
St Aidan's Technology College, Poulton Le Fylde

THE SNOWMAN

The snow lies thick upon the ground
Children laugh and play.
I go out and join the fun,
I'm out all day.
I build a snowman stout and tall,
With buttons for its eyes.
A twisted twig is for its mouth,
A tall hat proves its size.
I laugh to see it standing there,
It fills me so with glee.
But the others think I'm foolish,
And begin to snowball me.

Rebecca Wright
St Aidan's Technology College, Poulton Le Fylde

AUTUMN

Autumn leaves are crisp and chocolate brown.
They crunch beneath your feet
And make a crumbly sound.
They fall from the tree like a feather
In the cold and wet weather.

Autumn fires on Bonfire night glow.
Crackling and burning
As we watch the firework show.
They light up the starry sky
As the people gather by.

Georgina Newstead (13)
St Aidan's Technology College, Poulton Le Fylde

SMUGGLING

I was in the living room
Warm near the fire
When I had the urge to look into the gloom
There he was holding a barrel.

There he was staggering past
What was he doing?
And why so fast?
There he was shouldering a barrel.

I was so desperate to know what he was doing
So I crept out shivering into the night
He was very intent alright, no fooling
There he was heaving a barrel.

I crept ever closer, as quiet as a mouse
Peering ahead into the mist
He crept around the back of the house
There he was rolling a barrel.

I heard him hum an Irish song
Then my mother was behind me and she exclaimed,
'You've been smuggling all along!'
There he was trying to conceal the barrel.

Thomas Kelsall (12)
St Aidan's Technology College, Poulton Le Fylde